Living in
QUEBEC

HENRI DORION   NATHALIE ROY

PHOTOGRAPHS BY PHILIPPE SAHAROFF

Flammarion

CONTENTS

WELCOME TO QUEBEC

Quebec started out as a fortuitous encounter between explorers and a river, an encounter in the northern regions between France and North America, witnessed by the indigenous population. Then Ireland and England came, followed by people from everywhere around the world. There was far too much work to be done on this vast land and everyone lent a hand; winters lasted too long for settlers to remain at war for any length of time.

A brisk, lively language arose from the combination of all these outside influences. French words were livened up by the singsong rhythms of Ireland, while the British contributed a strict parliamentary vocabulary for one of the world's oldest democracies.

Welcome to Quebec.

When you open this book, you are opening a window on our own corner of North America: Quebec City, perched high atop the cliff of Cap Diamant, with copper roofs and an old walled town; Montreal, with its skyscrapers and bridges pointing in every direction of the compass; the immense landscape, where nature is so generous you can't help but be humbled.

"A time to sow / A time to wait / The gentlest autumns / Started in the month of May," wrote our poet Gilles Vigneault.

The climate and wide open spaces have forged the soul of a proud people. Quebeckers carry within them the warmth of our summers, the colors of our autumns, the determination of our winters, and the optimism of our springs. These same Quebeckers have drawn on this energy to build one of the world's most modern societies within the vast reach of our horizons.

Although this legendary and historical Quebec is still a fascinating place for Quebeckers themselves and visitors from the world over, it nonetheless stands firmly in the reality of this century. The Quebec of open spaces is also a land of science and research, and a world leader in several health-related fields. It is a high-tech society, a North American aerospace pole, and its expertise in the energy industry is recognized worldwide. Today's Quebec is a rich and diverse place. It encompasses all the cultures that have come together here in a hymn to peace and harmony.

Living in Quebec is a trip to this multifaceted Quebec, a voyage from the immense to the intimate. I would like to thank the authors, Henri Dorion and Nathalie Roy, who lent their hearts and minds to this book. I would also like to thank the photographer Philippe Saharoff for his astonishing images.

And, dear reader, I wish you bon voyage.

Whoever opens this book will certainly want to see and feel a unique North American experience: Quebec.

We'd love to see you here.

Jean Charest
Premier of Quebec

Water is inseparable from the Québécois landscape; it is a source of life. The St. Lawrence River was the port of entry for everyone arriving from Europe, "the walking path" for the First Nations, and the prince of rivers for the province's poets. Autumn in the Laurentians (page 1); during the summer, the brisk sea air is bracing in Port-au-Persil (page 2); at Baie-Saint-Paul, facing the Île aux Coudres (page 4), the river slowly washes past the banks. Tributaries flow into the river from the thousands of lakes in the backcountry of the Laurentian (page 6) and Appalachian mountains. Lighthouses and beacons mark the river's path from one end to the other (right).

LANDSCAPES

HENRI DORION

THE LAND OF WIDE OPEN SPACES

The Parc National du Mont Tremblant in the Laurentians (preceding page). The Eastern Townships south of the Saint Lawrence Plain (facing page, bottom) are less forested than the Laurentians (facing page, top), but offer more harmonious rural landscapes, with many covered bridges (above).

Living in Quebec means accepting a triple reality that underlies the charm of this land: the vast expanse of its territory; its character, which is far more Nordic than its geographic location would suggest; and, of course, the unique temperament of its residents. Some Quebeckers feel they are the French people of North America, others are more like Francophile North Americans. Whatever the definition, Quebeckers are a people with French roots, heirs to British institutions, and a repository of cultural contributions from the four corners of the planet, living in a country that has been the home to Native Canadians, known here as the First Nations, for centuries. Inspired by their deep understanding of nature, inherited from the indigenous people, Quebeckers have been able to face and sometimes avoid the challenges posed by a difficult yet stimulating natural environment. We must also remember that the province is made up of farmers who have become city-dwellers in the space of just two or three generations.

The surface area of Quebec is three times the size of France, but with eight times fewer people. Space takes on a different meaning in this context: for the Quebeckers who are, in fact, basically urban, everything outside their familiar territory constitutes something of a "nature reserve." Don't forget that four out of every five Quebeckers lives in a city. Nevertheless, most of them stay in touch with the outlying areas, lakes, and fishing camps. They maintain a constant desire to go over and beyond the mountain, and would like their visitors to do the same. Quebec is a land of many resources, both human and physical. The beauty and grandeur of these landscapes fully justifies its unanimously recognized nickname: la Belle Province.

A visitor from Europe will discover, on stepping out of the airplane, the very heart of the country, its core and its zone of maximum density. This is the large metropolitan area of Montreal, home to nearly half of Quebec's population. But if this same visitor follows the path of the explorers, either by boat or even in his mind, and approaches the country by the wide St. Lawrence River, he will imperceptibly follow the transformation of the sea into a gulf, then an estuary and finally the river itself, the "the walking path," as it was called by the Native Canadians. He will see a long string of more or less deserted islands between the gentle and seemingly empty undulating countryside. Forests stretch as far as the eye can see. The edges of the islands are dotted with a few villages. The towns start to appear farther, much farther upstream.

This itinerary will show the traveler that the words "space," "countryside," and "settlement" have distinct meanings on this side of the Atlantic. Visitors will make a first contact with the regions which, beyond the generous continuity of shapes that characterizes all of them, are differentiated by extremely distinct geographical features. The St. Lawrence flows through the middle of a long triangular plain that narrows downstream and disappears at Quebec City. The river separates the Laurentian Mountains to the north and the Appalachian Mountains to the south. Along its way, it washes through the metropolis of Montreal and the capital city, Quebec. It is also a region in and of itself, with its own personality and countless islands dotted along its passage. Living in Quebec also means embracing the colors and rhythms of each region.

It's well known that time moves at different rhythms depending on the region and the latitude. Quebec is vast. Its southernmost region lies at the same latitude as Bordeaux, while the northernmost point is just 250 miles (400 kilometers) from the Arctic Circle. Hence the seasons, like the length of the days and nights, vary considerably from one region to another. In the north, the dominant rhythm swings from long, late summer nights to winters plunged into long-lasting semi-darkness. In June, when night falls on the St. Lawrence Valley the Nunavik region is still gleaming in the sunshine of the white nights. In January, the white mantle that covers the north reflects the pale light of the sun for only a few hours, and sometimes just a few minutes.

The dimensions of the territory are such that the climate also varies widely, both in terms of temperatures and precipitation levels. The Îles de la Madeleine, smack in the middle of the Gulf of St. Lawrence, enjoy—or suffer, depending on the seasons—the temperate climate of the coast, while 310 miles (500 kilometers) to the west, the Abitibi region, the Siberia of Quebec, is known for its record cold temperatures.

Every season—whether it be the two seasons of the Inuit, the six of the Native Canadians, or the four inherited from European tradition that reign throughout most of the world—has its own rituals, colors, and popular lore. Quebeckers have adopted the rhythm of the seasons with an imagination richly nourished by their traditions. The climate is rigorous and demanding. The cold, the storms, and the snow banks are followed by the sometimes catastrophic and sometime joyous thaw of the rivers and the demonstrative frenzy of the short summers, with one last ephemeral return to warm weather signaled by the Indian summer—all essential elements of the art of living in Quebec.

A few acres of snow? Voltaire's *dismissive description in Candide underestimated the grandeur of this land, and also its wealth. Winter has been tamed and the tourists, like the Inuit, lead by huskies, skate along the frozen lakes. The river has been channeled, marked, and lined with towns and villages. There is water everywhere to prove it—in the middle of the forest (preceding pages), in the Gulf (left), and in the heart of the city (above).*

THE ST. LAWRENCE OR THE RIVER OF A THOUSAND ISLANDS

Les Îles de la Madeleine echo the thousands of islands that dot the St. Lawrence, an ultimate upsurge of the continent in the middle of a gulf that is as large as a country: remote houses between the sand dunes and the sea (preceding pages), lighthouses, and smokehouses (facing page), and shipwrecks and small harbors (above) contribute to this unique environment.

The St. Lawrence River, or "the walking path" as the First Nations called it, is the backbone of Quebec. It was the river that led the first explorers inland and is still the main, if not the only, shipping waterway in eastern Canada. The surface area of its basin, which includes the Great Lakes, is three times larger than France.

The St. Lawrence is a major force. By the time it reaches the territory of Quebec, via the gates of Montreal, it has already come a very long way. When it flows in front of Quebec City, under the walls of the Château Frontenac atop Cap Diamant, it still has a long way to go before reaching the Atlantic Ocean. By this point it has become a vast estuary. It then grows into a full-fledged gulf with a surface area of 77,200 square miles (200,000 square kilometers).

It is a highly changeable river. By the time it reaches the province of Quebec, it has already dropped many hundreds of feet, most spectacularly at Niagara Falls in Ontario. From here, it slows down in several places, forming a number of peaceful lakes. When it reaches Quebec, it widens to form Lac Saint-François, and then Lac Saint-Louis when it reaches Montreal. Halfway between Quebec City and Montreal, it expands once again, slowly, into Lac Saint-Pierre. The river is filled with year-round traffic as freighters chug upstream as far as Montreal, and—since 1959 and the creation of a major canal system, the St. Lawrence Seaway—as far as Toronto or Chicago. During the summer, the waterway is dotted with sailboats. The nearly constant wind makes this a prime sailing area. The combination of work and pleasure, rugged ocean-going vessels and elegant sailboats, creates a unique, vibrant environment.

It is a fairly stable river, with the exception of a few rapids around Montreal, then some very small ones slightly upstream from Quebec City. It is most noticeable for its ebb and flow. The tidal variations correspond to its scale; indeed, the river rises and falls an average of ten to thirteen feet (three to four meters), rising as much as twenty feet (six meters) in Quebec City. The spring tides sometimes even flood the streets of Quebec City's Lower Town.

The many rivers that feed into it, gathering almost all the runoff of southern Quebec, make the St. Lawrence the granddaddy of all waterways. It is the undisputed master in Quebec, not only for the size of the cities and towns that line its

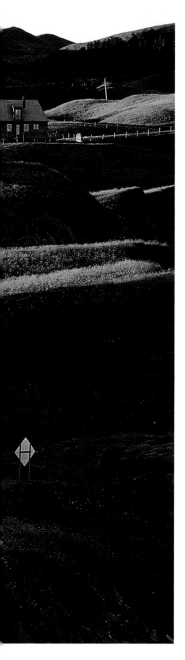

The relaxing island life is reflected in the seemingly aimless paths that wind between the dunes, partially covered with grass (left). There is little wood here, except for the houses and churches, like the church at La Vernière, which is said to be the largest wooden church in North America (right).

banks, but also because it forms a unique environment with thousands of islands along its passage.

The two largest islands in the Quebec section of the St. Lawrence are different in every way. The island of Montreal in the southwest corner of Quebec has some two million inhabitants. The 3,090-square-mile (8,000-square-kilometer) Anticosti Island, however, at the far eastern edge of Quebec, where the estuary joins the sea and the river become a gulf, is covered with forests and has no more than 300 residents and a herd of over 100,000 Virginia white-tailed deer. Two different islands, two different worlds. The river's path is filled with hundreds of other islands. Around Montreal, islands large and small form an archipelago which echoes the name of the waterway that links the St. Lawrence to the Ottawa River—the river of the Thousand Islands. This built-up string of islands is totally different from another group of islands farther downstream: the hundred islands of Lac Saint-Pierre, which form a strange oasis of undefined and intertwined channels flowing around easily flooded islands. This amphibious region is home to the largest heronry in North America and attracts both nature lovers and hunters, although the latter are strictly controlled. It's Canada's own bayou, the Louisiana of the North.

A few islands downstream from Quebec City are fairly large and graced with fertile land. These long, narrow islands mirror the farmlands lining both banks of the river at this spot. The Île d'Orléans is just a few minutes downstream from the capital. It still has a rural feel to it, where vegetable plots, orchards, and vineyards form a pastoral backdrop to the villages that have preserved the island's traditional old buildings. The churches, chapels, manor houses, houses, and barns belong to six villages, all located along a forty-mile-long (sixty-kilometer) circular road. This route offers an overview of the architecture, landscape, and farmlands of one of the best-preserved rural regions of Quebec. The island is a lovely counterpart to the Côte de Beaupré on the north shore of the Saint Lawrence; this coastline winds around a long string of architectural ruins of Nouvelle France (the North American territory under French administration prior to 1763) as far as Cap Tourmente.

The Île au Coudres has many similarities to its larger sister, the Île d'Orléans. Situated some sixty miles (one hundred kilometers) downstream from Quebec City, it still has a certain number of historical sites and craftsmen. It is located in the

On the Île aux Grues, fishing-boats and geese have inspired wood carvings (above). On the islands, no house is ever very far from the sea (facing page).

estuary section of the river, which explains why its traditional activities have always been, up to a decade ago, based on the sea: fishing and the construction of *goélettes**, the schooners immortalized in Pierre Perrault's film *Pour la suite du monde* (*For Those Who Will Follow*). Several of these *goélettes* are on display at the maritime museum in Saint-Joseph-de-la-Rive, opposite the island.

The Île Verte and the Île aux Grues, closer to the south shore, are also two little worlds that reproduce the conditions and traditions of farmers along the St. Lawrence plain, although within an isolated and therefore more self-sufficient environment. Many of the homes are now second residences, but these landmarks of times past preserve the relaxed atmosphere where the bracing sea air combines with the gentle, easy pace of the traditional rural landscape.

As the river flows downstream, the islands increase in number and become more diverse. Some, such as Grosse Île, have served specific purposes. It was a quarantine station during some of the most tragic immigration periods in Canadian history. Thousands of people, primarily Irish, died of typhus after the difficult ocean crossing. Many other islands are occupied by lighthouses, each manned by a single keeper; they marked the difficult passages for ships traveling upstream. A lot of these sentinels along the St. Lawrence are still operational. They are poignant reminders of the maritime exploits of the early explorers.

Many islands were also used as bases for the Gulf fishermen, who built modest homes on these rocks battered by the waves. Others, those opposite Kamouraska, for example, await in silence the return of the bird hunters or those who collected the down from the eider ducks. Still others have never seen any visitors other than shipwreck survivors or sailors abandoned to their fates on some deserted island—all stories that feed the local legends and ghost stories. Who knows? On a foggy or full moon night, they just may rise up and leave the hundreds of sunken ships that are strewn over the bottom of the river around the Îles de la Madeleine, the Îles de Mingan, and, especially, Anticosti Island, nicknamed the cemetery of the Gulf. Don't worry about taking any of the coastal boats, though: navigation along the St. Lawrence is now completely safe.

The islands in the St. Lawrence form a symphony of infinite tones. Upstream, the phrase "one island, one city," reflects the geographic reality. An undefined and amphibious archipelago of islands at the end of Lac Saint-Pierre offers an entirely different and extremely serene landscape. Downstream from Quebec City, the few outposts of rural tradition are the exception in this long string of islands in the St. Lawrence. Even farther east, the still forested oblong-shaped islands echo the peaks of the Appalachian Mountains. The sedimentary rocks of the Îles de Mingan have been eroded into creative shapes by the sea and the wind into a geomorphologic garden: some seem to represent flowerpots, women, silhouettes of Native Canadians, mushrooms, and more. At the end of the trip, as the river nears

the Strait of Belle Isle, where icebergs from Greenland float past every springtime, even the small and inhospitable rocky islands have not deterred small populations of fishermen.

The constellation of the St. Lawrence islands forms a distinct world characterized by diversity and dispersion. Yet they all share certain features. In the middle of "the walking path," the days and the seasons go by at a pace that differs from the rhythm on the two riverbanks. They have acquired a long history that is slow to change and is well worth your while to explore.

After its long trek through Quebec, during which the St. Lawrence offers a spectacular backdrop for memories, legends, historical events, images, and landscapes, the great river adds a friendly postscript: the Îles de la Madeleine. This string of islands is a lovely jewel right in the middle of the Gulf of St. Lawrence, closer to the Atlantic provinces than to Quebec. Its remote location, practically outside the province, is naturally one of its unique features. The islands follow a different time from the rest of Quebec both symbolically and literally, as it is located in a different time zone.

No two houses are the same on the islands, but they all have similarities: non-geometric layouts, simple shapes, sloping roofs, bright colors, and wood everywhere.

And yet mainland Quebeckers love these islands so much that many, far too many perhaps, want to move there either permanently or for the summer. Nevertheless, the islands have preserved an authentic charm. Sea and sand come together here to create a landscape that can't be found anywhere else in North America, combined with a climate that is exceptionally mild for this region.

This land is unique in that most of the islands are interconnected by long sandbars that have created a total of a hundred and eighty miles (three hundred kilometers) of beaches. Given the favorable climate, it's not hard to imagine the attraction of these islands. To get a good idea of what they're like, you have to go to Butte du Vent to see what the sea and wind have created in tandem. From here, you can observe the long sand spits and lagoons, which stretch out over forty miles (sixty kilometers) in a series of dunes, beaches, cliffs, inlets, and caves that surround this linear landscape.

The names of the islands clearly reflect the landscapes: Grand Barachois (Large Sandbar), Buttes Pelées (Bare Buttes), Chemin des Échoueries (Shipwreck Path), Cap aux Meules (Millstone Cape), Anse aux Étangs (Pond Cove), Anse du Moulin (Mill Cove), Île Rouge (Red Island). They also evoke the diverse animal life that thrives here: Bassin aux Huîtres (Oyster Basin), Île aux Loups-marins (Seawolf Island), Île aux Goélands (Seagull Island), Anse des Baleiniers (Whalers' Cove), and Baie Seacow.

A few houses are scattered in a seemingly haphazard pattern on these treeless bits and pieces of the continent. Views of the wide-open landscape include the omnipresent sea, which fills the horizon. The continent cannot be seen from any point on the islands as it is sixty miles (one hundred kilometers) away at its closest spot. The gentle shapes are highlighted by the island's own distinct colors: the blue sea, the red cliffs, the yellow dunes, and the green carpet of the soft waving grasses—along with the wide range of bright colors the residents have chosen for their homes.

Structures that rarely exist anywhere else in Quebec anymore can still be observed in these islands, such as the sheds with sliding roofs which protect the hay from the weather, boat docks, and drying barns. It's a rare pleasure to see more boats than cars: fishing boats of all sizes, rowing-boats, and other small craft are constantly moving in and out of the bays and lagoons. Ferries from the mainland appear at regular intervals at the Cap aux Meules docks, as do smaller boats that ply the route to the Île d'Entrée. During the summer, the islands are surrounded by kayaks, inflatables, motorboats, and sailboats taking summer residents and visitors on tours of the caves, cliffs, dunes, and beaches.

The island's most valuable and endearing resource is its population, many of whom are descendants of an Acadian population who took refuge on these sandbanks to escape the *Grand Dérangement** in the mid-eighteenth century, when the British authorities controlling the area deported nearly all of the Acadians (who were living in what is now Nova Scotia).

Blue sea, white geese, red cliffs. The Île aux Grues (above) and the Îles de la Madeleine (right) offer a wide palette of colors, as do the houses themselves.

Since then, the islanders, who have retained the Acadian accent, have lived off the sea, which has provided them generously with lobsters, scallops, crab, and other fish—although many of these species are threatened by the large appetites of the seals that have proliferated in the gulf since public opinion turned against the seal hunters.

An increasing number of summer residents and retired people have increased the numbers of the original inhabitants. Indeed, ironically, there are more native Madelinots* in Montreal than on the islands, while more and more city dwellers from Montreal and Quebec City are seeking the peace and quiet of the islands. It's easy to understand why: the islands are poles apart from the frenzy of urban life, and offer a wide range of landscapes, colors, historical references, products, and activities that all contribute to this surprising, original and unique world. It's food for thought, if you're thinking about traveling here before this paradise has changed too much.

THE APPALACHIAN MOUNTAINS

After stretching across a distance of 1,550 miles (2,500 kilometers), the Appalachian Mountains drop into the St. Lawrence River, forming the islands and peninsulas of Bic (preceding page) and the Parc Forillon (above and facing page).

The Appalachians form the southern border of Quebec. It is a gentle and relative barrier, as these mountains are not excessively high and are lined with valleys, making communication fairly easy. This is a land that alternates between wooded mountain crests and small valleys, which in the western region are mostly agricultural. The transition between the St. Lawrence Valley and the Appalachian Mountains is a gentle one. As the highway leaves Montreal and winds toward Sherbrooke, for example, it first passes through an absolutely flat plain, then gradually starts to wind upward. The foothills and rolling hills are gentle at first, then become more distinct. Once past the piedmont, the road curves through the crests that are aligned in a southwest-northeast direction, which is characteristic of the Appalachians.

This mountain chain, which runs diagonally across the entire territory of Quebec located to the south of the St. Lawrence plain, is the continuation of the longest mountain range running along the eastern edge of the North American continent. It extends from Alabama in the south to the eastern tip of Quebec, known as the Gaspé Peninsula. This long chain of mountains varies widely, starting a large crescendo from its entrance into Quebec south of Montreal, gradually growing higher as it moves eastward. The mountains end in steep rocky summits and spectacular views of the Gaspé Peninsula.

Life in the southern regions of Quebec is largely a function of the complex history that has subjected this region to a fairly constant movement of its population. This has created an interesting variety of people and traditions. The Eastern Townships as far as the Beauce region, the Lower St. Lawrence, particularly Kamouraska, and the Gaspé Peninsula form three distinct regions that each deserve a separate introduction.

The Eastern Townships are located in the southwest corner of Quebec. This apparent paradox can be explained by the history of Canada. During the eighteenth century, the system of townships first developed in what was then called Upper Canada. It was then expanded to Lower Canada, in other words, eastward, to Quebec, hence the name Eastern Townships, also knows as Les Cantons-de-l'Est or L'Estrie.

This is one of Quebec's most scenic areas. The climate is moderate; the land is gentle, although a few mountains are high enough for some downhill skiing. The forests are inviting, less dense and less wild than in the Laurentians. Nature seems to be tamer here; indeed, agriculture is a major activity in this region. The people

live here in natural harmony with the site. It's no accident that a group of Benedictine monks chose the peaceful banks of Lake Memphremagog for their monastery, where their chants blend in with the inspiring sounds of the surrounding countryside. In a certain sense, the Eastern Townships are an extension southward of the fertile lands of Quebec, with the advantage of forests in which the plant life, particularly deciduous trees, is far more diverse than in the north, where coniferous trees are more common.

This is wood and pasture land, where man has covered the piedmonts with vast orchards, supplementing nature's initial gifts. It's a generous land with abundant groves of maple trees, a symbolic tree that was tapped for maple syrup even before the Europeans set foot in the New World. Today, maple syrup producers have become large-scale, thanks to new processes that have made the industry more profitable—doubtless to the detriment of local color and the charm of using the original rudimentary instruments that produced such a rich, colorful, and precise vocabulary. The tractor has of course replaced the horse, and the maple trees are hooked up to tubes like patients on IVs. Nevertheless, these modernization procedures have not altered the festive feeling around the sugar shacks, from which rises a perpetual fragrant smoke that is like nothing else in this world. During the sugaring season, thick columns of blue smoke rise up in the spring skies. For everyone nearby, this is a quiet sign that it's time to come celebrate and savor the maple taffy*.

Agricultural production in this region has been diversified and there are now some wonderful routes to follow in search of these products. The wine route crosses through a number of vineyards growing different varieties of grapes; the quality is improving with every year. Quebec is certainly most proud of its cheese route: cheese production in recent years has achieved a level of quality that rivals some of the world's best.

It's clear to see that it has been human intervention that has given this region its unique character. The history of the area's occupation is the opposite of what occurred elsewhere throughout Quebec. During the British conquest in the mid-eighteenth century, the French-speaking population primarily moved to the land north of the St. Lawrence River, leaving uninhabited the more hospitable foothills of the mountain chains to the south. Hence, when the British arrived, they settled in this region. Later on, the Loyalists, those who retained their allegiance to the British crown, also moved here when the American Revolution got under way.

These new settlers developed the region according to their own specific structures. The land divisions, based on districts, were different from the system of long lots and rows set up by the French speakers. The tidy, clean homes in the districts and the careful landscaping around them are similar to New England houses. The large number of churches and chapels also reflects the diversity of

Religious or not, travelers cannot resist the serenity and tranquility of a visit, or even better a stay, at the Benedictine monastery at Saint-Benoît-du-Lac, where the monks are both farmers and musicians (above and left). Here the soft folds of the Appalachians along Lake Memphremagog echo the rise and fall of their chants.

Quebeckers have a special fondness for covered bridges, and about one hundred have been conserved and maintained on secondary roads. They are a reminder of the good old times when horse-drawn carriages had to follow such signs as "No trotting allowed." The red bridge of Grande-Vallée on the Gaspé Peninsula blends into the landscape admirably well.

religious practices in the Protestant world. Some villages, even small ones, have three, four, and even more religious buildings of various styles—although the neo-Gothic style predominates.

The place-names often illustrate the region's specific nature. In the St. Lawrence Valley, almost all the villages have French names, while as soon as the visitor nears the first foothills of the Appalachian Mountains, the language changes, with English names taking over—even though in the last few years there has been a strong movement to gallicize many of the place names. The most striking example of this phenomenon is the town of Sherbrooke; it was originally English-speaking, but the population is now ninety percent French-speaking.

The Beauce region is situated farther to the east. This name was a deliberate choice, as the first residents to this generous land wanted to emulate the Beauce area in France, known as the country's breadbasket. In time, their dream would unfold differently in this new colony, where the settlers pursued diversified agriculture, combined with orchards, dairy farms, and a large number of maple groves. The Beauce is watered by a river, the Chaudière, and is one of the most beautiful regions of Quebec, where the mild climate and agricultural diversity create a pleasant lifestyle.

The Kamouraska region, halfway between the Eastern Townships and the Gaspé Peninsula along the axis of the Appalachian Mountains, is a lovely coastal plain. This is where the last folds of the Appalachians roll down and submerge into the river. Small hills, which are known locally as *cabourons**, rise up here and there throughout the lovely agricultural land, most of which is devoted to the production of grain. These hills are dotted with pretty houses built in the traditional architectural style of the region. These *cabourons** are one of the interesting geographic features of the Kamouraska: they are in perfect alignment with the direction of the Appalachian folds as far as the river, forming capes, then *tombolos* (sand-spits), and then islands as they extend into the water.

Continuing downstream, the road leads to Bic, which has the same terrain of hills and valleys as the countryside farther west, but starts to become more rugged, offering a taste of what is to come farther along in the Gaspé Peninsula. Farther to the east, the landscape, people, architecture, and lifestyles change. The sea is much closer and its impact considerably greater here: as the hills and mountains get higher, agriculture decreases and the farming villages are replaced by fishing villages. The forest and mountains have taken over; the land here is much wilder and untamed.

According to tradition, every Quebecker feels that he or she must "go round the Gaspé" at least once in their lives. This is meant quite literally, because the Appalachian Mountains are at their highest on this peninsula, forcing the residents to live along a narrow coastal strip wedged in between the sea and the

In the Eastern Townships, single trees have personalities that don't stand out in the immense boreal forests. They often stand alone and, as here, adorn English gardens created in the region settled by British immigrants. The architectural style imported to this rural region from the nearby United States has resulted in unique structures, such as round or octagonal barns. The overall effect is one of a harmonious countryside—and is popular with Montrealers.

Two landmarks stand at the far eastern edge of the Gaspé Peninsula, the end of the Appalachian Mountain chain: the Rocher Percé and the Île Bonaventure, which is home to a colony of northern gannets.

mountains. Like the north coast, the inhabited area is linear. Yet behind this inhabited section lies a wealth of plant and animal life, along with the peaks and landscapes that make this area a budding haven for tourists—as well as an economic lifeline for an economically troubled region.

There was a time when fishing was a thriving and generous industry for a majority of the local residents. Seals, however, are extremely voracious and have considerably decreased the stock in this gulf—as has the fishing industry itself. The peninsula's residents therefore started to develop their many and diverse tourism resources. Mont Jacques-Cartier rises 3,865 feet (1,268 meters), making it the second highest mountain in Quebec. It is just one of the many dramatic peaks in the Parc de la Gaspésie, offering hikers breathtaking views over the spectacular landscape. The people of this high plateau often remind mountain lovers that an essentially Nordic environment can also exist in the south of the country, as the high altitude makes up for the lower latitude. Roe deer, moose, and caribou share this still remote region—an almost antique phenomenon that draws visitors hoping to see all three species.

Many rivers tumble down the steep slopes from the central plateau toward the St. Lawrence River, while others, on the southern side, flow more gently into the Baie des Chaleurs. This name reflects the existence of a pleasant microclimate that is protected from the north winds by the Gaspé Peninsula. This feature means that the long beaches are much more attractive than those on the north side, where it requires a good dose of courage to leap into the water. Spas also dot the seaside along this coast, a reminder that the Gaspé Peninsula is a sea environment where the scent of algae and kelp is never very far away.

The chief activities on the Gaspé Peninsula are fishing, hunting, and art. Several of its rivers, the Matapédia being the most important of them, have a series of salmon pools shared among fishermen according to a long-established attribution process. But in this land of long winters, imagination and crafts also play a major role. Indeed, the local craftsmen create a unique kind of work, inspired by the many legends that nourish the local traditions. After the Kamouraska region, where wood sculpture reigns, sea motifs gradually take over as the primary theme. You may be offered a wide selection of miniature sailboats in bottles, the ubiquitous souvenir of the Gaspé Peninsula, or a number of whalebone sculptures.

At the end of the road, at the farthest tip of the peninsula, is the famous Rocher Percé, or pierced rock, in the town of Percé. This last gasp of the Appalachians is one of the best-known landmarks in Quebec. The spectacle continues with the sounds of crashing waves and the impressive colony of northern gannets, which live along the high cliffs of the Île Bonaventure. Be sure to see this rock, walk along the paths, and observe the stunning chunk of limestone from all possible viewpoints. It's a breathtaking end to this last land of Quebec.

THE MOUNTAINS AND FORESTS NORTH OF ST. LAWRENCE

The only way to reach most of the thousands of lakes in Quebec and discover the region of Mont Tremblant (preceding pages) or Charlevoix (facing page) is by float plan. Hikers through the forest can look forward to the local specialty: blueberry pie (above).

The images of Quebec are well-known: infinite spaces, interminable forests, the silence of northern wilderness areas, the Aurora Borealis, and vast snow-covered fields. You only have to travel a short distance away from the St. Lawrence plain and its network of cities and towns to discover the geographic reality that the Quebeckers simply call the North, an immense region that extends from the St. Lawrence plain to the Arctic emptiness. This area represents ninety percent of Quebec's land. With the exception of two inland basins, Abitibi and the region around Lac Saint-Jean, this region is a sea of mountains; the peaks seem to roll on and on in long green waves, turning to blue as they reach the distant horizon. This landscape seems to go on forever, with deep trough-shaped glacial valleys cutting through the rocky mountains. This is also a land of water, with nearly a million lakes among the profusion of moraine deposits. These lakes represent nearly one-sixth of the surface area of Quebec.

It's therefore no surprise when locals say, with only a slight exaggeration, that "every Quebecker has his own lake." Where else on earth could, "I have a lake for you," be used so aptly as a declaration of love, as the poet Gilles Vigneault has one of his characters say? And who wouldn't be delighted with one of the three hundred Long Lakes as a site for a fishing camp? These lakes were created in Quebec as a result of glacial erosion. Or one of the hundred Round Lakes, relics of the late ice packs that dotted the territory? The names of the many lakes in Quebec are derived as much from their colors as from their shapes: along with Lac Violon (Lake Violin), Lac en Coeur (Heart Lake) and Lac Culotte (Shorts Lake), the maps are filled with names reflecting the three primary colors of the North. Indeed, the number of Lacs Verts (Green Lakes), Lacs Blancs (White Lakes), and Rivières Noires (Black Rivers) is legion.

The lake-mountain-forest trilogy is the major characteristic of this region. Northern Quebec consists primarily of endless forests; the southern region includes both deciduous and evergreen trees, gradually giving way to spruce trees farther north, followed by the taiga and finally, the tundra of the Arctic wilderness. The Inuit land between the St. Lawrence Valley and the Nunavik territory covers a region three times larger than France. The immense Laurentian forest was once

The decks of the many cabins surrounding Lac Sacacomie (left) are perfect spots to dream about the wide open spaces and the mountains that extend beyond the hills that surround the lake past the Laurentians toward the interminable north reaches. The Native Canadians mixed bearberry (Arctostaphylos uva-ursi), *which they called* sakakomi, *with their tobacco. The road leads up hill and down dale to many other lakes (right).*

considered to be an endless resource—until ecologists began to realize its relative fragility and promoted more reasonable and sustainable development. Not everyone is convinced that even this is the right policy to follow, and indeed some people have called the massive logging of the forests an "error borealis."

The First Nations had a symbiotic relationship with these forests and a far more extensive knowledge of the language of this indigenous flora and fauna. Water diviners and bone readers knew how to interpret this language and found in it a source of predictions and techniques. Traces of fire on animal bones led them to the lair of whatever game they were seeking. With their expertise, they could transform white birch, whose bark is waterproof and rot-proof, into tents, boats, various types of receptacles, quivers, and *tikinagans** (cradleboards

for carrying infants, embroidered with beads and brightly colored patterns). Boutique shops in most of the reservations—and in Montreal and Quebec City—offer a selection of these objects, souvenirs of a past when self-sufficiency was the norm. You can also purchase a dream-catcher*, which is meant to be a filter between the imaginary world and reality.

Europeans have learned much from the Native Canadians. Up until the nineteenth century, houses in the country were often insulated with birch bark, a material used for Iroquois and Huron longhouses. This was not the only technique they borrowed: others include snowshoes, sleds, canoes, and dogsleds. The methods developed in the North require the use of certain tools that any visitor can learn, even if it's just for the duration of a single excursion. Locals even organize workshops in traditional hunting techniques. If you're looking for something out of the ordinary, this is the place for you. You'll be more than welcome.

Settlers and colonists who arrived later wanted to exploit the country's forestry resources, and the construction and pulp-and-paper industries brought in masses of loggers, who exiled themselves for months at a stretch cutting down the boreal forests. Temporary lumberjack camps sprang up all over the territory. Hikers can sometimes see traces of these camps in the forests, but they are fairly far off

the logging roads, some sixty, one hundred and twenty or one hundred and eighty miles (one, two or three hundred kilometers) from any signs of habitation. Most Quebeckers, used to the large open spaces and long distances, would consider this to be a small excursion. The techniques in the forestry industry have relegated the traditional log rafts to the past, although the trainloads of logs that you may encounter on certain banks of the north side of the St. Lawrence are reminiscent of the era when the log drivers used to skip nimbly over the floating rafts of timber.

The northern forests are rich in animal life, notably moose, roe deer, bear, and caribou. Wolves and lynx are more unusual and infinitely harder to spot. The northern stretches of Quebec have always been prime hunting and fishing grounds for Native Canadians and the Inuit, who still depend to a certain extent on these activities for their food. It is also a favorite hunting and fishing reserve for many southern city dwellers, although it's now possible to fish almost directly in the city, and trout-stocked ponds are everywhere. A few clever game farmers have enclosed caribou, roe deer, boar, and even the majestic elk within fences where hunters can easily shoot their prey.

When the month of October arrives, the forests fill up with hordes of hunters who all hope to bring home, if luck is with them, some venison to last through the winter—and if they catch a moose, the antlers are displayed over the fireplace or entryway. Don't be surprised if you see a car disguised as a moose, driving down one of the backcountry roads or even in the city, for that matter: the owner attaches it as a roof ornament as proud evidence that he brought down the one animal he was allowed to kill per year. The hunting season also opens in July for another animal, this one a miniscule but overwhelmingly annoying creature: Canada's famous mosquitoes. One of the major topics of summer conversation concerns surviving these pesky creatures. The best way is to cover all exposed skin.

Northern Quebec is a vast reserve of plants, animals, minerals, and energy resources. It's a challenging land where man has conquered immense distances and a rugged climate, a land that has retained much of the original mystery of its large open space

Temporary, nomadic villages exist not only in the Sahara Desert. Every winter, villages of small houses spring up along the white desert of Quebec's lakes and rivers. Their modest exteriors belie a surprising level of comfort, with wood stoves, couches, and televisions making the sporting life somewhat easier. A few brave souls do without shelters for ice fishing.

and the untamed beauty of the northern regions, a country within a country, without which Quebec would not be Quebec.

But there are many different northern regions and each one is distinct from the others. There is the area north of Montreal, the so-called Laurentians, although technically this term applies to the entire mountain range that continues north to the west of Quebec City, where it reaches it highest altitudes. This area north of Montreal has also been nicknamed Les Pays d'en Haut, an expression that reminds some of the older Canadians of the most popular radio program in all of Quebec's history, *Un homme et son péché*, inspired from Molière's play *L'Avare* (*The Miser*), a story about a not-so-distant time when Quebec was still a pioneer outpost.

Compared with other northern regions, this area is considered an "almost northerly" place, an outlying forest of lakes and hills where many city dwellers seek out a peaceful refuge after a long work week or even at the end of the day. The most active enjoy water sports during the summer and skiing during the winter. The ski resorts here are among the largest in Canada and attract an international clientele. But it's also a great place to relax and many retired people have moved here.

The busiest highway in Quebec, especially on Fridays, links Montreal to this popular vacation area. The road replaced the small Northern train that nevertheless remains etched in the memory of many—and in a song by Félix Leclerc. The former railway line, which has now acquired a legendary status, has been turned into a bicycle trail that runs past nice little stations as it goes from village to village. Many of these stations have been renovated tastefully and transformed into tourist inns, without losing any of their former charm.

The Ottawa region farther to the west is something like an extension of the Laurentians in the Montreal area. Their tail-end lies in the Parc de la Gatineau, created by the Commission de la Capitale Nationale du Canada, although this park is highly organized—almost overly so—apparently for pedagogical reasons. Panoramic trails and overlooks offer great views over the city of Ottawa, the Ottawa River and the surrounding countryside. The old homes provide historical interest; the oldest of these is the Mackenzie King house, where the picturesque and the mysterious come together in a tribute to the longest-serving prime minister in Canadian history.

The Laurentians to the east offer an entirely different experience. La Mauricie is the homeland of the granddaddy of Québécois songwriters, Félix Leclerc. It's therefore logical that one of his favorite themes was the forestry industry,

Liberty, Eternity, Trinity, Equality, Fraternity: this litany of evocative and majestic names reflects the majesty of the capes they designate along the Saguenay Fjord (left). In Quebec, you have to protect yourself from the snow, even on the bridges.

The Parc du Mont-Tremblant also has its own romantic author. "I have a lake for you," sang Vigneault to his love. Others have their own islands, a sentimental getaway in the great forest garden of the Laurentians.

particularly the log drives and the logging camps that he sang about with such realism and poetry. One of the largest rivers in Quebec, the Saint-Maurice, flows through this region. For many years, it was the route by which the timber cut in the backcountry was floated downstream to the city of Trois-Rivières, the world's leading city for the production of pulp and newsprint. Drivers no longer float the logs down the river; they are now transported by road via long lines of logging trucks. They are a reminder to the people farther south that their northern hinterland is an Eldorado of rich forests. Despite all the logging activity, this is a beautiful road that winds through a magnificent landscape of water and trees.

An immense wilderness area separates Quebec from the Saguenay region, which with the Lac Saint-Jean forms a territory crisscrossed by large rivers, all of which empty into the majestic Saguenay fjord. The Réserve Faunique des Laurentides was created to conserve the ecological balance that was threatened by intensive logging. This overuse had resulted in the disappearance of caribou and salmon in the area. Thanks to its status as a protected area, the flora and fauna now thrive in a harmonious environment that offers a haven for hikers, vacationers, fishermen, sportsmen, and researchers.

The Parc de la Jacques-Cartier next to the reserve is a perfect example of a characteristic U-shaped glacial valley. If you love mountain hikes and have the energy to climb the steep paths running through the park, you'll be rewarded with breathtaking views.

Once autumn arrives, the spectacular colors of the forest make this extraordinary landscape seem almost unreal. The gorges of the upper Malbaie River offer an equally magnificent setting.

The higher altitude of the Parc des Grands Jardins, which has been named a UNESCO Biosphere Reserve, means that the park has the climate of higher latitudes. The primary vegetation on the Mont du Lac des Cygnes is that of the tundra, where a carpet of multicolored moss and lichen covers the ground. This environment forms a natural habitat for caribou. These animals had practically disappeared from the area due to over-hunting, but they were reintroduced into the reserve and the herds have now reached a stable population. The caribou appear to be

Downstream from Quebec City, where the Laurentians plunge directly into the St. Lawrence River, the magnificent combination of sea and mountains illustrates the superhuman dimensions of the region.

Charlevoix offers year-round activities, depending, of course, on the whims of nature. Winter has its own unique characteristics: the "white ceremony" as sung by Vigneault, the bluish tint of the pure cold light on the snow, the long shadows cast by the low-lying January sun, and the sharp relief. Nature generously warms the hearts of Quebeckers.

almost tame, as do the gray jays, which often drop by to visit campers and nibble off their plates.

The majestic Saguenay fjord, the "Gate to the Kingdom" as it's called, marks the start of the Côte Nord that extends to the eastern edge of Quebec. This region does not change that much between the Canadian Shield and the river, although it does have a string of small deserted islands. The towns are farther and farther apart along the six-hundred-mile (thousand kilometer) coastline; even so, the entire population of this area is concentrated along the water, while the inland region is a no-man's-land.

The long coastal road stops at Natashquan, the birthplace of the singer Gilles Vigneault, who set the legends and characters of the Côte Nord to music; this is a land outside time. The fishermen are the only ones to fathom all the secrets of this region that is covered in fog and battered by offshore winds most of the year.

It took the release of a recent film, *La Grande Séduction*, filmed in the village of Harrington Harbour, to unravel a bit of the mystery surrounding this handful of houses perched atop a rocky outcrop off the inhospitable coast. It's an almost entirely unknown area, as it can only be reached by boat or airplane. Although it takes a determined traveler to reach it, the unique Côte Nord is certainly worth the effort.

Most city dwellers consider this to be a lost land, yet a more remote region lies even father to the north. This is the territory of Nunavik, the land of the Inuit, where the rhythm of the days and nights is replaced by slowly shifting annual seasons, from nearly twenty-four-hour-a-day sunlight in the summer to semi- or total darkness in the winter. This is far beyond the usual tourist paths, yet it has its own charm, which is as rugged as the climate, as strange as its landscapes. During the winter, beyond the northern limit where trees no longer grow, the rocks are totally bare, except for a few *inukshuks**, stone monuments made to look like human beings. During the winter, it's impossible to distinguish the ground from the sky; everything, in all directions, is white.

If you have a desire to discover the extraordinary land of Nunavik, you'll have to make the necessary arrangements to reach it. Airplanes provide the only access to the villages and can also fly you over the crater of Nouveau Québec, a circular lake, two miles (three kilometers) in diameter, created by a meteorite. If you want to explore outside the villages themselves, you can travel by dogsled or snowmobile during the winter, or ATVs in the summer. But summer is a short season in the

land of the Northern Lights, a one-month frost-free period.

Nevertheless, the land stretching north of the St. Lawrence Valley is far from being just an expanse of impenetrable forests and tundra. Despite the rugged geography, this region has been visited, inventoried, mapped, mined, and logged for a long time. Furthermore, nature has provided it with two enormous oases that offset the monotony of the northern forests. These are the Saguenay-Lac-Saint-Jean (which some people call Sagamie) in northern Quebec, and the Abitibi-Témiscamingue in northwestern Quebec.

A ring of clay-like soil around Lac Saint-Jean supports a fairly prosperous agricultural industry; the thick forests are also an economic resource. This is the land of blueberries, known in Québécois as *bleuets**, and the *ouananiche**, an indigenous species of fish similar to a trout. The Jeannois* (residents of Lac Saint-Jean) are known for their imagination and joie de vivre. Like the Saguenay region, this area has many festivals and carnivals. Every autumn, the locals are invited to share a huge blueberry pie. They say it's a record-breaking size, which is a good thing given the traditionally large families in the region. True or not, the six-foot (two-meter) diameter pie is a good reflection of the generosity of the Lac Saint-Jean residents.

There is also an annual swimming competition that attracts participants from many different countries, who race across the lake. The Bleuets (the name for the locals), fishermen, hunters, and Innu*, with whom they share this territory, love to explore deep within the forests in search of the best trout-fishing lake, the best salmon pools, and the best spots for moose. No one is one hundred percent urban at Lac Saint-Jean.

The same thing can be said of the Abitibi, which carries the nickname "the Siberia of Quebec," not only for its climate, but also because of its range of resources. Different ones have been more highly prized than others over the years. It was initially the realm of the fur trade, and then attracted the interest of the forestry, pulp and paper, and mining industries. Here, as elsewhere in the enormous Canadian Shield region, the land is predominantly forested. If you fly over this sea of greenery, which is crisscrossed by the blue and ocher ribbons of the great northern rivers, you get an idea of the immensity of this challenging land of the future. But for a truly existential experience, drive along the twelve-hundred-mile (two-thousand kilometer) road linking Montreal to Caniapiscau. Not recommended for those who don't like long distances, solitude, and silence.

The boreal forest covers most of the surface area of Quebec. Despite its seeming uniformity it offers a large range of assets. In the backcountry of the Côte Nord (left), it consists almost exclusively of coniferous trees, while deciduous trees occur more frequently in the western regions, which are more accessible. Horse-drawn trips around Lac Sacacomie (right) are a great way to enjoy the winter.

QUEBEC CITY
A PROMONTORY OVER THE RIVER

Quebec is a two-tiered city. The Château Frontenac on the promontory stands proudly above the landscape of Quebec City, viewed from Lévis (preceding page), its turrets (above), or from the Petit-Champlain neighborhood (facing page).

Of all the nicknames used to describe Quebec City, "the Gibraltar of America" is certainly the most representative both in terms of its site and its location. Quebec's capital reigns proudly atop a headland, the last one narrowing the St. Lawrence before it opens up into the estuary that, from this point on, flows widely toward the sea. This is how the Native Canadians viewed this site when they named it Quebec, which means "the river narrows here" in the Algonquin language. The name Cap Diamant dates from the era when Jacques Cartier explored the region; he discovered quartz crystals and believed, mistakenly, that they were precious stones. East of the cape, the St. Lawrence is already starting to resemble the sea: the water is salty and the river's width rapidly increases tenfold. This is reflected in the names of the villages: Berthier-sur-Mer (Berthier on the Sea) and l'Islet-sur-Mer (Island on the Sea). Upstream, the river is narrow enough for bridges. There are two near Quebec, one at Trois-Rivières. These are the only three bridges downstream from Montreal—which is still more than nine hundred miles (fifteen hundred kilometers) from the Atlantic.

The narrowing of the river at Quebec City underscores the strategic location of the city, situated at the intersection of Quebec's three large geographical regions. An exceptional observation point offers a spectacular view of all of them and gives the visitor an overall idea of Quebec's general makeup. From the capital's observatory, placed atop the city's highest building, a 360-degree view spreads out over the gentle blue mountains: the Laurentians to the north and the Appalachians to the south. Looking to the west, you can see the plain extending to the distant inland regions. This is Quebec's farmland, home to most of the agricultural activities. Toward the east, beyond the Île d'Orléans, a lovely pastoral haven just past the city, the riverbanks start to recede from each other, as the river flows out over the wide estuary dotted with a myriad of islands. Some of these stand alone, others are part of archipelagos.

From Dufferin Terrace, a long walk that follows the edge of Cap Diamant from the Château Frontenac to the top of the Citadel, you can get a closer look at the flow of the river and its banks. During the short summer months, sailboats leave the marinas and fill the river with white sails. And in the winter, foreign visitors will be surprised to see the ice floes in the river float upstream, then downstream: they change directions four times a day, according to the tidal flows. In Quebec

Nouvelle France, Vieille France, Place Royale, Louis XIV: is this really North America? Quebec City looks a little like Saint-Malo and La Rochelle in France. At least, that's what Quebeckers think, happy that Quebec City has conserved the intimate ambience of French towns better than anywhere else in Canada. The best place to start a tour of Old Quebec (left) is at the Place Royale, with its bust of Louis XIV (right).

City, the tide rises more than ten feet (three meters). Throughout the entire year, the ferry linking Quebec to Lévis across the river sails past freighter ships steaming up the St. Lawrence toward the Great Lakes. During the warmer months, luxury cruise ships make stopovers in front of the Lower Town, just below the Château Frontenac. For a few hours, thousands of tourists pour off the ships for a rapid visit. This, too, is a continuation of Quebec's long-lasting maritime tradition. The shipyards at Lauzon near Quebec City are another reminder of this history.

The British probably viewed Quebec as a new Edinburgh because in both cities, the center overlooks densely populated neighborhoods that stretch out at its base. Quebec City is actually a city with two levels, a fact reflected by the everyday use of the names Upper Town and Lower Town. But the city also has intermediate areas and especially pedestrian corridors. These are the many stairways that climb the hill forming "Quebec island," and that clearly follow its contours. The Upper Town is proud of its churches, archdiocese, and government institutions. The Lower Town is closer to the less attractive area of past and present industries, where the tanneries and shoe factories were once a predominant part of the urban landscape. Shipbuilding was also a major industry.

Just like in the houses, the different levels of the city can be recognized by their respective functions. The ground floor comprises the entrance and services; upstairs belongs to the masters of the house. From its earliest days, Quebec City seems to have reproduced this vertical separation of classes that characterizes a number of other cities as well, including Budapest, Prague, and Geneva.

When the city was founded four centuries ago, the mother of Quebec cities was, because of its site and location, a key strategic position for the European powers who gradually transformed it into a fortress as assault followed assault, battle after battle. If you're interested in military architecture, you'll enjoy exploring the walls with their four monumental gates, circular fortified towers, military manege, artillery pieces that were never used, Artillery park, barracks, redoubts, garrison, and large Champs de Bataille park. All of these monuments form a unique environment that has been placed on UNESCO's World Heritage list. Visitors are often struck by the military installations of the city, yet Quebec has not seen any warfare in 250 years.

Today, this city seems much more romantic that military, particularly with the proud Château Frontenac. This imposing structure was constructed at the turn of the twentieth century to house travelers from the Canadian Pacific Railway Company.

Quebec is a peaceful city. The cannons lined up along the ramparts have never been fired (above). The Terrasse, between the Château Frontenac and the river, is on a strategic military site; summer and winter, it is one of the favorite meeting places for locals.

It was designed something like a castle, with angle towers, overhangs, corbels, carriage gateway, and courtyards. The interiors are in keeping with the overall design: royal suites, antique furniture, ballroom, tapestries, and coats of arms illustrate the lavish fashions popular during the great era of the Canadian railway. This splendor is the result of a great adventure that gave rise to its own unique style; indeed the Gare du Palais in Quebec City and the Gare Viger in Montreal share a distinct family resemblance.

It's said that the Château Frontenac is the most widely photographed hotel in the world. It is certainly inseparable from the city's image. Viewed from any angle, it is impressive for its size and its old-style architecture, which is exceptional in Canada. Its signature shape, clinging to the edge of Cap Diamant, looks its best from the Place Royale in the Lower Town, narrowly wedged in between the cliff and river. From this viewpoint, it looks like a craggy citadel.

Despite the many vestiges of its military past, its former function as a garrison town has not made Quebec City an austere place. Quite the contrary: Quebec is a great city for strolling, exploring, and meandering, particularly because of its old stones, steep narrow streets, backyards, and vistas overlooking the river from its many belvederes. People walk, meet, and play in the fields and military structures where conflicts—either real or projected—once justified their construction.

This is the case with the Parc des Champs de Bataille, although peaceful Quebeckers prefer to call it the Plains of Abraham. This is where the future of Canada was played out during the 1759 conquest of Quebec. Today, it is a vast haven of greenery where people play sports, come to enjoy concerts, and attend the many cultural events. There are always people here, every time of the year. Parents take pictures of children astride the now silent cannons. During the winter, they career down the slopes on makeshift sleds. Behind the military manege, the city organizes international ice sculpture competitions. And at the base of the walls, behind the Château Frontenac, a long and vertiginous ice slide is a popular thrill with everyone, young and old. Every year, during the famous Winter Carnival, Quebec City is graced with a new ephemeral structure: the ice palace, whose translucent form contrasts with the austere ramparts, creating a general headquarters for the carnival's fun and games. The two-week carnival is filled with festivities, parades, and contests.

The long wall surrounding the old town for about two and a half miles (four kilometers) no longer protects anyone against anyone else. It is now a wonderful site for a walk, and families and couples follow the rampart walk to discover the unique poetry of the city's rooftops. An immense landscape stretches out from the Rue des Remparts between the carefully aligned cannons, with a long thin strip of houses known as the Côte de Beaupré, the site of the very first settlement

Quebec City, with its ramparts and gates, has a slightly medieval feel (with a little imagination). Every winter, Quebeckers create ice castles suggesting other imaginary sites of the Great White North (facing page).

in Nouvelle France. You can continue exploring this panorama from Dufferin Terrace, which offers views over the south bank and the upstream section of the St. Lawrence. The Québécois have adopted the Spanish tradition of the *paseo*: it's said that Dufferin Terrace, Rue Saint-Jean, the Grande Allée, and the Plaines are prime sites for lovers. Perhaps these stimulating landscapes provide the inspiration for budding love affairs?

A walk through the streets of old Quebec City offers the promise of other types of encounters: fascinating rendezvous with history.

Everyone agrees that Quebec City is the cradle of the French presence in North America. But its distinctly French character—easily confirmed by the fact that ninety-five percent of the population today is French-speaking—has gone through difficult times in the past, in a different ethnolinguistic context. Indeed, the city's diverse architecture is visible proof of this. One century after the conquest, in other words, in the mid-nineteenth century, half of the population of Quebec City had become English-speaking. Today, the buildings are living testimony of the two languages, with the history of successive loyalties: to France, to the British Empire, to a French-speaking country, and to modernity.

In Sillery, a suburb of Quebec City, the Vieille Maison des Jésuites, which many historians believe to be the oldest house in Canada, recounts the history of the Jesuit missionaries, some of the earliest French arrivals on this soil, who came to convert the First Nations. Nearby, a Native Canadian cemetery is a discreet reminder of the country's original inhabitants.

Very early on, members of other religious orders arrived to devote themselves to the spirits and souls of the people living here. The Séminaire de Québec, the oldest institution of higher education in Canada, was created several decades after the city itself was founded in 1608. It is one of the essential and emblematic sites of the old capital. A beautiful gate and carriage entrance lead to a courtyard that is worthy of this temple to knowledge and devotion: the venerable, all-white walls seem to have been frozen in time, while a highly secular sundial hanging on one of the façades indicates the hours. It seems to watch over the calm serenity of this place that appears to be separated from the time and space beyond its walls.

Successive additions have transformed the buildings into a complex that includes a college, chapels, a reliquary, and a museum illustrating various facets of the French population in America, including its history and culture. The Université Laval was located here until the early 1960s. The shape and color of each element of this complex are distinct historical examples of their times. Professors in the architecture department of the Université Laval, which was moved back here when the other departments were transferred to Sainte-Foy, several miles from the center, therefore have examples right at hand to explain the development of

styles in Nouvelle France. Quebec City also has its own Latin Quarter and small cafés where students meet to remake the world between classes.

The monks from the Séminaire also bequeathed to posterity other structures inspired by the same architectural sources. It's lovely to stroll through the pathways of the Domaine de Maizerets, not far from the downtown area. The property has farm buildings constructed in the eighteenth century and is a rare example of rural architecture from this period. Farther away and even more impressive is the Domaine du Petit Cap, at the base of Cap Tourmente. The eastern edge of this rocky outcrop terminates the St. Lawrence Plain. A very well preserved architectural complex on the cape overlooking the river includes several period structures, notably a lovely chapel.

Nouvelle France experienced troubled times before peace was finally reached with the Native Canadians in the west and the British in the east. It was a long process. A small chapel, the aptly named Notre-Dame-des-Victoires, set on the Place Royale, has a bust of Louis XIV; its name refers to two historical events that delayed the British conquest. In 1690, when an emissary of Admiral Phips summoned the Comte de Frontenac to hand over the city to the English, the reply was brief: "Tell your master that I will answer with the mouths of my cannons." No sooner said than done, and the French won the first round. Natural elements came to the aid of the colony in 1711, when the tumultuous waters of the St. Lawrence engulfed almost the entire fleet of Admiral Walker during a storm. The second round went to the French. Visitors to the Place Royale can't help but feel a spirit of the old French here.

But despite these victories, the French were ultimately conquered. Quebec City was bombarded and many were killed or wounded. The Hôpital Général des Soeurs Augustines, which also housed a convent of nuns, is located in a building in the Lower Town. It is a reminder of the important role played by this congregation during the Franco-British War. Don't miss a visit to the small museum, which keeps alive the memory of this era, as does the Mémorial de la Guerre de Sept Ans (Memorial to the Seven Year' War), recently inaugurated opposite the hospital.

Winters in Quebec are harsh, but fun. Viewed from Lévis, Quebec City stands out magnificently against the ice (preceding page). Snow underscores the relief of the monuments, as on the Place d'Armes (left). It also paves the way to the Fresque des Québécois, a mural depicting four hundred years of Quebec history (right).

Quebec City is a good place to test your fitness: twenty-seven staircases link the two levels of the city. The Casse-Cou staircase (facing page, top right) is the oldest and climbs to the Upper Town from the Petit-Champlain neighborhood (bottom left). Small houses with dormer windows dating from the period of French rule line the streets of the old districts (top left and bottom right). The house of Louis Jolliet, who discovered the Mississippi, is one such house; the funicular leading to the Terrasse (right) starts here.

The British made a considerable contribution to the physiognomy of the city founded by Samuel de Champlain. The walls, fortifications, citadel, and a number of defensive structures started by the French were completed by the British. Several Scottish cottages still exist in the city and its outskirts. Recently, distinct tributes were added to the Scottish (la Chaussée des Écossais) and the Irish (the Celtic Cross). A look at the street names of Quebec City reveals a long list of figures from the two empires that battled over the site. Alongside Jacques Cartier, St. Louis, Henri IV, and Napoleon are Wolfe, Dalhousie, Sutherland, and even Moncton, although he was the one responsible for the deportation of the Acadians. The rivalries between the two colonies are eloquently inscribed in Quebec City's place names. Visitors from both England and France will often encounter references to their own country.

But with the passage of time, Quebec City has become more and more French. Place de la Francophonie and Parc de l'Amérique française are new sites in the urban landscape. Locals and visitors come together every year to celebrate the Fête de la Nouvelle France. Even the old buildings reflect these changes. Hence, in places on the old stone walls you can see street names in French that have been recently painted over the faded English names.

Like any other interesting city, Quebec is worth taking the time to visit, stopping to examine the street corners and the street signs that indicate the origin of the names. Pause in front of the frescoes depicting the history of the city, wander around to peek into some backyards, and climb up one of the long staircases from the Lower Town to gradually, step by step, appreciate the haughty charm of the Upper Town.

If you're interested in seeking out unusual sites, take a look at the smallest street in North America, Rue Sous-le-Cap, which crosses over a series of passageways, or catch a glimpse of what is said to be the narrowest house in North America, on Rue Donnacona. Be sure to climb up the pretty pedestrian Rue du Petit-Champlain, underneath Cap Diamant, where you'll find a string of shops that give you a good idea of the innovative nature of the Quebeckers. Don't think that the name of this cute little alleyway was in any way meant to diminish the status or image of Quebec's founding father. In Quebec, people often slip back and forth from one language to another; hence, Rue du Petit-Champlain is a literal translation of the English Little Champlain Street.

The Rue des Antiquaires, properly known as the Rue Saint-Paul, is an antique lover's dream situated in the Lower Town. If you're interested in art, make a trip to see the artists and artists-in-training who hang their drawings and canvases on the walls of the Rue du Trésor in the Upper Town. You might almost believe you're in Montmartre. Quebec City also has its own miniature Champs-Élysées: the Grande Allée, which offers a selection of restaurants and cafés filled with civil servants at lunch—not surprising, given that several ministries of the provincial government are located nearby. In the evening, this is a popular meeting place.

The residents of Quebec City take advantage of their terrific location at the crossroads of Quebec's major geographical regions. The Laurentians are nearby, providing nature lovers with a land of lakes and mountains swathed in the calm that only the northern forests can give. The moose, roe deer, and bear are close to the city, and indeed, can sometimes be seen in the city itself. At dusk on summer nights, there are guides who can take you to listen to a truly unforgettable sound: the howling of the wolves.

The mountains morph smoothly into the plains in the outlying areas of the capital. All that marks this shift is a long strip of waterfalls hemming the edge of the plateau. There are dozens of them around Quebec City. The most impressive, Montmorency Falls, is an ostentatiously abundant display of white water cascading over a cliff two hundred and sixty feet (eighty meters) high. Locals are proud to tell you that they are one hundred feet (thirty meters) higher than Niagara Falls.

During winter months, the mist from the waterfalls turns into snow and forms a mound of ice nearly one hundred feet (thirty meters) high—to the delight of visitors who bring along sleds and sleighs to play on this slope. There are also a number of ski runs in the area, and hundreds of miles of cross-country ski trails in the Laurentian Mountains above Quebec. The rugged contours of the Canadian Shield have also produced some prime downhill skiing facilities, notably at Mont Sainte-Anne, Mont Tourbillon, and Stoneham.

The Place d'Armes is a lively place in the summer. In the winter, it slumbers under the snow, awaiting the return of tourists who come to admire the prestigious monuments around the square: the Château Frontenac, the Anglican cathedral, the former courthouse, the former main post office, and the pretty Maillou house dating to the era of French rule. There's plenty here to inspire the artists who exhibit their canvases on the Rue du Trésor, adjacent to the square.

MONTREAL'S INDEFINABLE CHARM

The Montreal skyline with its play of vertical, horizontal, and circular lines (preceding page and right). A few reminders of past centuries remain, such as the Hôtel de Ville (town hall, above) with its Second Empire style.

All the ingredients of a major city—a core of skyscrapers, an expanse of outlying dormitory towns, a tangle of urban freeways, traffic jams, long distances—all those elements that are often considered to be nuisances can be found in Montreal. Yet this city has an undeniable charm, though it's hard to actually define it. Some people have totally fallen under the spell of Montreal; for others, it's not quite such a sure thing. Poets and songwriters have praised the unsuspected beauties hidden in courtyards and small streets, in the shadows of the overwhelming structures or lost in faceless suburbs. And the expression "macadam flowers" used to describe the lovely young Montreal women is perhaps a good reflection of the paradoxical attraction of this large city.

What makes Montreal such a popular destination for people from all over the world? Is it the many monuments, scattered throughout a fairly uniform urban landscape? Or do so many travelers come here for the cultural life and large number of festivals, museums, cosmopolitan spirit, tolerant atmosphere, thriving economy, parks, and restaurants—not to mention the many Canadians from other regions who have decided to settle here? Perhaps it is the multi-faceted nature of the city, with ties to France, the United Kingdom, Canada, the United States, and South America that confers on it this mysterious magnetism.

Montreal is often called "the city with a hundred bell towers." Does it still deserve this nickname? Many cities around the world could be given the same name, and in Montreal, these vertical landmarks of religious art are increasingly disappearing in the shadows of the temples to the new religion, business, with skyscrapers housing major banks and multinational companies. Nevertheless, these bell towers, at least the ones that remain, reflect the diversity of religions, which mirrors the ethnic complexity of the city itself.

In fact, Montreal does not really have a clear image. It is not an emblematic city; it does not have a distinct architectural character or exceptional natural setting, like Quebec City, Victoria, or St. John's, which would make business easier for the postcard companies. Younger than Quebec City by a quarter of a century, Montreal grew more quickly thanks to its advantageous geographic location. Immigration from diverse countries has enriched the city in many ways. Its cultural, economic, and social characteristics are more diversified, making it a place that encompasses many facets—and also makes it harder to grasp than Quebec City. Especially as the latter is a relatively homogeneous city, as opposed to Montreal, which is far more complex. The problem in defining Montreal's charm is certainly

One hundred and fifty years ago, the city started to construct the first bridge connecting the island of Montreal to the mainland. The 1.2-mile (two-kilometer) Victoria Bridge (right) was initially used only by the railroad, which first crossed the continent in 1885. The linearity of this bridge is offset by the elegant Jacques-Cartier Bridge (left), a cantilevered bridge that is one of Montreal's symbols, as well as a discreet reminder of Molson beer.

due to this composite makeup that is in constant flux. This dynamic city is liable to surprise anyone who's been gone for just a few months. You could almost say that Montreal is an event; indeed, its many festivals alone demonstrate this.

Montreal's location is nature's gift. The city occupies an island situated halfway between the Atlantic Ocean and the Great Lakes, and spreads to the banks of the largest river flowing into the North Atlantic; furthermore, this river is perfectly navigable up to the city. Montreal is also at the heart of a rich agricultural plain, which is an exception in this rugged land. All in all, Montreal is a prosperous place. Located 155 miles (250 kilometers) upstream from Quebec City, Montreal was protected from European invasions from the north. Others, however, arrived from the south. The Americans and Native Canadians attacked and temporarily occupied the town, underscoring the strategic importance of the site that controls the immense inland regions. But today, no more walls, no more fortifications commemorate these heroic times; they disappeared long ago.

To fully comprehend the insular nature of Montreal and the size of the river system that surrounds it—and to understand the importance of water in the development of the metropolis—take a boat trip on Lac des Deux Montagnes and Lac Saint-Louis. If you're attracted to water sports and don't mind getting wet, you might want to take a raft trip down the Lachine Rapids. It's a good way to get a feel for the turbulent water and the courage of the early boatmen, known as the voyageurs*, who crossed the continent by paddle and portage during the pioneering years of the colony. The size and power of Montreal's waterways illustrate the necessity for engineering projects that would make the city more accessible.

Montreal may be surrounded by water, but it is not isolated. Eighteen bridges link the city to the south bank and surrounding areas; five of them cross the St. Lawrence. One of these structures is as venerable as it is weatherworn. This is the Victoria Bridge, the first bridge built over the river, in 1859. The 1.2-mile (two-kilometer) span gives an idea of the river's width and impressive flow.

Until the opening of the St. Lawrence Seaway, Montreal was the river terminus and as such was an essential stopover point for the transshipment of goods. The harbor still has all its characteristics: the views of the southern shore and boats of all sizes, shapes, and provenance, lined up for miles, form a mainstay of the Montreal waterfront.

The other essential asset in Montreal's location is the beautiful mountain that rises in the middle of the island. The tree-topped summit stands out from the immense checkerboard of streets that surrounds it on all sides. The fresh air and great views from the top of Mont Royal are irresistible. Starting in the mid-nineteenth century, luxurious homes gradually began to climb up the flanks of the most urban of Montreal's hills and the source of the city's name. Locals concerned with the development soon came to the defense of the mountain and set about protecting it for the entire population of Montreal. Now it is a park forming an immense stretch of greenery complete with rocky outcrops, promontories forming lovely overlooks, a lake, and magnificent vegetation.

The park was created in 1876 and is a prime source of fresh air for the large metropolis. Throughout the year, this oasis attracts lots of visitors, who can observe many different kinds of animals at liberty: marmots, squirrels, raccoons, chipmunks, and seagulls can be seen as you wander along the paths. During the winter, the hills are a popular place to ski, skate, and sled.

Several viewpoints have been created on Mont Royal. The Chalet de la Montagne offers a spectacular panorama over the city, against a backdrop of the distant Appalachians. The downtown area in the foreground surges straight up to the sky, like a peak of a stone and glass mountain; this cluster gradually decreases on either side of the river toward the more horizontal lines of the south shore. This is where you can get a good idea of the size and density of Montreal. Another viewpoint farther to the east looks out over several of the hills in the outlying areas, far beyond the suburbs that seem to blend into the river and the islands.

The Montreal cityscape has it own unique dialectic. It consists of opposites, and each element seems to stand next to its opposite. The verticality of the downtown area contrasts with the horizontality of the outlying towns. The angular geometry of the office buildings is offset by large, rounded structures, such as the Biosphere, the Olympic Stadium, the Casino, the design of Pont Jacques-Cartier, several domes, Marché Bonsecours, and the Calder stabile, all of which soften the skyline. Another contrast: children play and couples stroll down the narrow streets as cars roar by on the dense system of highways that crosses the city. Montreal's charm would not be complete without both sides of this picture.

This city juggles with opposites on every scale. Underneath the stone megaliths that shoot skyward up to six hundred and fifty feet (two hundred meters) high is a network of underground galleries that link several shopping districts, office buildings, and apartment buildings, for a total of nineteen miles (thirty kilometers) of pedestrian passageways. Also connected to the Métro, they are used by many commuters on their way to and from work. The system is a great way to do errands, visit friends, and generally take care of business without going outside—which is no small thing during the glacial winter months. Here again is

An off-ramp from the Jacques-Cartier Bridge (bottom left) leads to the Île Sainte-Hélène, which with the Île Notre-Dame was the site of the 1967 World's Fair. Several of the pavilions were kept and readapted to new purposes, such as the Biosphere (right), a dome one hundred and ninety feet (sixty meters) in diameter that housed the US pavilion. The theme of the exhibition was "Man and His World," echoed by Calder's stabile, Man (top left).

Touring the city of Montreal is like touring the world (clockwise from top left): opposite the Hudson Bay Company store; British Lord Strathcona stands in the middle of Dorchester Square, named for an Irish-born governor of Quebec; nearby is the headquarters of La Presse, *the largest French-language daily newspaper in North America; farther along are Chinatown and the Marché Jean Talon with its many Italian shops. McGill College Avenue and Mont Royal (left) also reflect Montreal's bilingual identity.*

The Marché Bonsecours (this page) contributed to the changing face of the city. Constructed on the site of the former palace of the provincial administrator, this building was originally the city's first indoor market; it then housed the Canadian parliament, then the town hall, followed by municipal offices. Today it is a venue for exhibitions. The surrounding area is lively in summer and winter, while other stone figures populate the city in silence.

another paradox: while a large portion of the population hibernates underground like the bears, others, in the more working-class areas, have to clamber up the outside staircases of the buildings, which is more often than not a real challenge in the winter. The rows of staircases stretching along several streets form a strange-looking urban tapestry.

Montreal is a composite city in many ways, including its population. Its size is the chief factor, in that nearly one in every two Quebeckers lives in the Montreal metropolitan area. Ever since the British conquest, successive waves of immigrants have arrived, starting with the Scots and followed by Loyalists during the American Revolution. This result of all these populations is a highly diverse city that has managed to integrate all these new arrivals into the urban landscape. Can Montreal, like many other large cities, be called a "town with one hundred villages"? Yes and no.

The British presence that left its mark on the city starting in the early nineteenth century is visible in the Victorian architecture. This style has given a stately air to some of Montreal's neighborhoods; it's not ostentatious by any means, yet it creates a clear difference from some of the working-class neighborhoods populated mostly by Canadians of French descent, drawn here by the rapid industrialization of the city. These neighborhoods were soon filled up with long, British-style row houses. The French-speaking and Irish Catholic populations lived side by side, each contributing to the dichotomy that exists today in the socioeconomic map of Montreal, with the wealthy English speakers to the west and the less well-off French speakers to the east. Montreal has repeated a phenomenon that appears in many other cities, where the rich congregate in the west of cities: Paris, Budapest, Mexico City, Quebec City, Montreal.

The Quiet Revolution* was a period in Quebec's history in the 1960s that ushered in intense social change along with a rejection of more traditional, conservative values. This had a considerable impact, but many of the rifts of the time have healed. It was a time when Quebec claimed its French heritage. In 1830, the majority of Montrealers spoke English, but fifty years later, it had once again become a French-speaking city. Today, two-thirds of the population in the metropolitan region speaks French. This shift has been relatively slow, as each community has bolstered its ranks in its own way: the English through immigration and the French through high birth rates. Nevertheless, Montreal today is the second largest French-speaking city in the world after Paris, even though most of the economy still remains in the hands of the English-speaking segment of the population and the multinationals. Even with these two main populations, Montreal is still far from a homogeneous city.

The statistics speak for themselves: forty languages, thirty religions, and some fifteen hundred community cultural associations. But there's no need to consult the figures to realize just how multiethnic Montreal really is. All you need to do is

undertake a well-planned expedition through various neighborhoods and districts. All you have to do is pay attention to what you see, what you hear, and even what you smell, in order to get a vivid picture of the intricate ethnic mosaic of the city.

Little Italy, in Saint-Léonard, in the northeast part of the island, is clearly marked by a leaning tower that everyone recognizes. All around are a multitude of cafés. It's worth your while to stop and take in the local color and to explore the markets, where signs proudly display the words "Fresh from Italy today!" On the other side of the city, in Chinatown, specialty grocery shops on Rue de La Gachetière fill the streets with fragrant smells—although you can find Chinese restaurants scattered all over the city. Between Little Italy and Chinatown, the Portuguese have congregated around a square near Rue Saint-Urbain that boasts a pillory (not in use, fortunately) in the center.

Avenue du Parc, which runs along the eastern edge of Mont Royal, has a profusion of Greek restaurants, which reflects the size of this community here and makes visitors think of the Acropolis as they look up at the sky line. At Outremont and Snowdon on the western side of the island, a Hassidic Jewish population holds close to its traditions. The beautiful architecture of an Armenian religious and education complex farther to the north is a reminder of the importance of this community in the city's cultural life. And if you climb into a taxi, you're more than likely to have a Haitian driver from the north of Montreal.

Newcomers to Montreal do not all come from far away. Many of them arrive from the four corners of the province of Quebec. Everyone has his or her own reason: economic, cultural, family, or social. There are, for example, more people from the Île des Madeleines, known as the Madelinots, in Montreal than on the islands themselves. The Bleuets (from the Lac-Saint-Jean region) and many other regional populations have created associations to maintain links with their roots.

Is Montreal something of a League of Nations, where everyone has preserved his or her own characteristics, languages, food, and traditions? The answer is both yes and no. One thing is certain: this is anything but the American melting pot. On the other hand, when you walk into a simple restaurant, probably run by a Greek, you may easily see a menu vaunting "Canadian cuisine." The waiter may be Yugoslavian or Mexican, trying to learn French as he suggests, in broken English, spaghetti or smoked meat* (introduced to Canada via immigrants from the Baltic, although everyone believes it is a homegrown tradition). This mixture wouldn't surprise any Montrealer. It seems that everyone wants to fit into this Montreal blend which is part of the city's charm.

Montreal's botanical garden, one of the most beautiful in the world, is a delight for all five senses. The elegant Oriental art of gardening is magnificently displayed in the Chinese and Japanese gardens; visitors leave these havens fully restored. The explosion of colors in the tropical greenhouses offers surprising sights. Even your taste buds can participate: the Insectarium serves up insects to visitors.

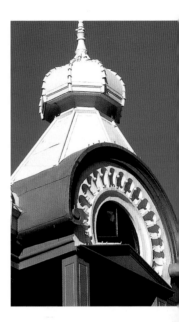

Montrealers must be prepared to confront the winter with these houses featuring outside staircases. Saint-Louis Square (known locally as Carré Saint-Louis) offers the most beautiful example of this architectural style which exists in many cities throughout Quebec. This small park is the cultural heart of Montreal. Students, residents, intellectuals, and cultural communities of all kinds gather here, under the picturesque Victorian façades.

Montrealers may love their neighborhoods, but they'll also venture out to others. There's a multitude of impromptu and planned meeting places. For shopping, the four-mile (seven-kilometer) Rue Sainte-Catherine lives up to its reputation with large department stores and small shops. But, like everything in Montreal, there's no hard and fast rule. If you explore the street from west to east, you'll move from an upscale neighborhood to a working-class one, from trendy stores to secondhand shops, from well-heeled preserve to a bustling, cheerful ambiance, from luxury to lewdness as well—Montreal also has its share of vice, as does every big city.

Once spring has fully arrived, which in Montreal is usually a week or two before Quebec City, the cafés and patios fill up. It's a well-known phenomenon: popular spots for pleasant encounters and serious discussion tend to be in the same areas. Rue Prince Arthur and Rue Mont-Royal both have dozens of restaurants, forming an uninterrupted line of temptation. But it's Rue Saint-Denis that beats all the others. The multifaceted main artery runs through Montreal's Latin Quarter. Lovely nineteenth-century houses have been converted into trendy shops, bookstores, and bistros. Students from the Université du Québec à Montreal (UQAM) add to the constant flow, combined with disparate groups of people that make this street a linear agora that is unrivaled anywhere in Quebec. The new Grande Bibliothèque (Main Library), now under construction, is located nearby, and will also certainly add to the energy, with people sitting for hours on end, sipping coffee and reading a book even if all they're doing is pretending to be bohemian intellectuals.

For another type of encounter, head to one of the many museums and galleries, or the Botanical Gardens, which are the second largest in the world, where you can enjoy an unusual meal of insects or one of the other creatures on the menu. There are also the parks, which have earned Montreal the nickname of the Green City: the family-oriented Parc Angrignon, the Parc Jarry for the more sports-minded, the popular Parc Lafontaine, and the fun Parc Sainte-Hélène.

And speaking of green spaces, Montreal is not very far from its two inland regions: the Laurentians to the north and the Appalachians to the south. Some Montrealers consider it their backyard, an extension of their urban home. Others go there for a necessary alternative to the bustling life in this city of three million inhabitants, in search of a tranquil haven from a city that is anything but.

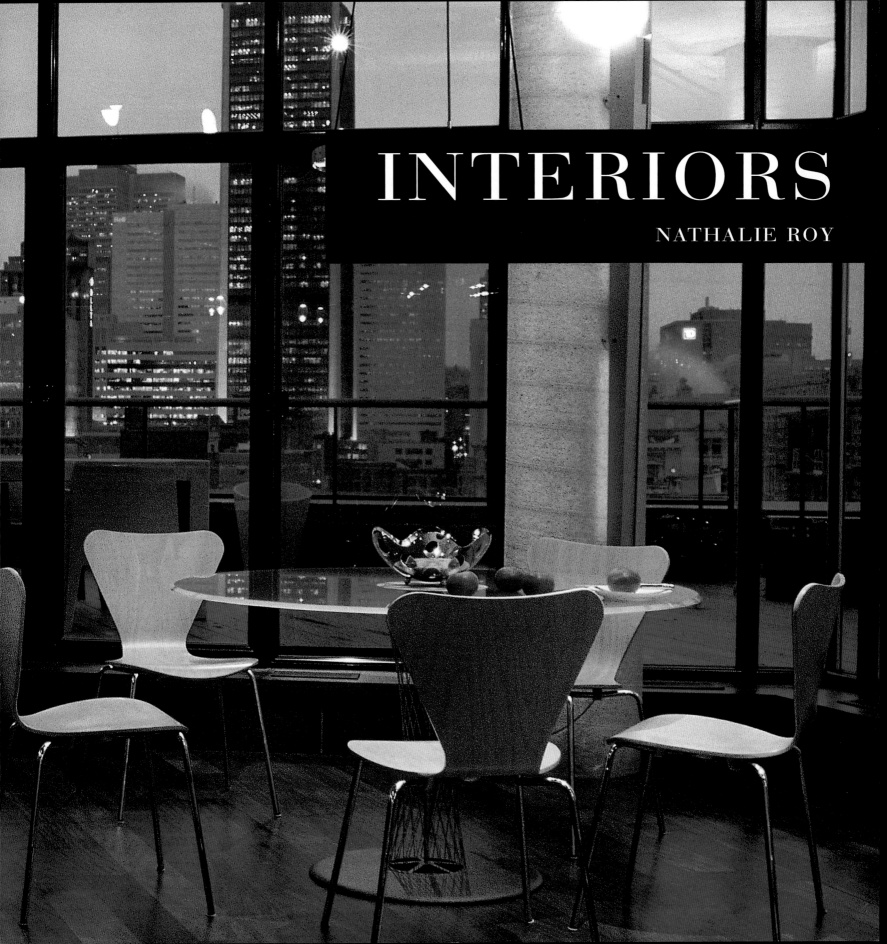

INTERIORS

NATHALIE ROY

LIVING IN QUEBEC

This apartment overlooks Montreal's lively downtown area (preceding pages). Habitat 67 provides an escape while remaining within the bustle of Montreal (facing page, top). A log cabin in the Laurentian Mountains illustrates the pioneering spirit (top), while another in La Mauricie reflects contemporary Quebec (facing page, bottom).

Quebec is a land of many traditions, which is clear even in its architecture. The Québécois home often combines several different styles that have been adapted to political or climatic conditions. This amalgam, known as vernacular architecture, is an original interpretation of the successive French and English governments, along with the trends and tastes that fashioned present-day Quebec. Discovering its architecture means dipping into history, from the pioneers, with the log cabin of designer Jean-Eudes Desmeules, to contemporary Quebec, with the villa in La Mauricie created by architect Pierre Thibault.

Architectural styles are also regional. In the Eastern Townships, for example, designer Johanne Dunn's property reflects the specific characteristics of New England homes; the Saint-Louis house, on the other hand, has been adapted to modern tastes by designer Serge Lafrance and is representative of Montreal's Victorian past. The Havre-aux-Maisons residence, designed by the architects of the YH2 agency, includes an outbuilding, a feature often seen on the Îles de la Madeleine.

The steeply sloped roof was common in the eighteenth-century French colonial style and is still visible on Île d'Orléans. The roof angle softened somewhat during the eighteenth century and became longer in the nineteenth century with the arrival of English and Scottish immigrants. This roof extension marked the start of the covered porch (a practical feature when there's a lot of snow), which is a characteristic of English classicism and many American homes. The country cottage then appeared, built for urban dwellers as summer residences. The cottage transformed into a single-family bungalow with one or one and a half floors; this design has become common in the city, suburbs, and even the countryside. The Montreal triplex is another regional design. These houses have picturesque external wrought-iron staircases, a result of the dense urban fabric (and the fact that they were less expensive to construct). It has been successfully adapted to the small bungalow transformed into a tower house by the YH2 architects.

Everything seems to undergo a metamorphosis in Quebec: churches become luxurious residential complexes, while schools and other public places are transformed into charming private homes, such as that of Martin Gagnon—or ever more offbeat, the factory-loft belonging to designer Jacques Bilodeau.

This overview would not be complete without mentioning Habitat 67 in Montreal. The stack of concrete cubes, an experimental project by Moshe Safdie, a young architecture student at the time, reflects major modern movements in architecture. Even today, Habitat 67 is still highly prized for its exceptional quality of life.

HABITAT 67, A SYMBOL OF MODERN MONTREAL

"Intelligence means creating links between things which on the face of it don't seem to be linked."

Christian Mistral

This living room in a Habitat 67 apartment in Montreal is straight out of the 1960s (facing page). The curved furniture and decorative objects in the bedroom soften the geometrical lines (above).

Habitat 67 is an experimental residential complex by Moshe Safdie, designed when he was still an architecture student, for Expo 67, held in Montreal. This array of cubes, which each contain one or two rooms, is still as popular as ever.

It's 9:30 A.M. The noise of the nearby city is muffled by the turbulent rapids of the St. Lawrence River. "This morning, my wife and I went shopping at the Atwater market on our bikes," smiles the owner.

Habitat 67 is just a few minutes from downtown, yet it offers the charm of the river, a small park and a large network of bike paths. The configuration of cubes creates different landscapes for the occupants, and for this professional couple, who work in the legal field, the apartment includes two floors and has no grass to mow—thereby combining the advantages of an apartment and a house, without the disadvantages of either one.

Books, classical music, and contemporary art are the inspirations for the styles developed by the YH2 architects, Marie-Claude Hamelin and Loukas Yiacouvakis. "It's stimulating to imagine taking the architect Safdie's major idea even further," says Yiacouvakis.

A highly personal style

The owners look at architecture as if it were a work of art. They take good care of their home and they like YH2's idea. "Initially, we were only going to remodel the living room, as my wife and I didn't like it at all. It was neither pleasant nor practical," notes the owner, who has been at Habitat longer than almost anyone else: he moved here in 1969. The couple quickly became enthusiastic about redefining their space in terms of their current needs, while respecting the original Habitat philosophy.

The result is a Mondrian-like composition, a variation on the theme of boxes within boxes. "We returned to the idea of the 'block,' with its own identity, in which each mass is related to another," explains Loukas Yiacouvakis.

The three cubes were redesigned according to function and balance. The music corner, for example, which was next to the kitchen, was transformed into a guest room and office, while the cramped office space on the upper floor became a closet space, as the logical extension of the master bedroom and bath.

In this Habitat 67 apartment, art offsets the cubic form. A bronze piece in the bedroom creates a gentler look (left). The work by Québécois painter Pierre Ayot adds a cheerful note to the meditative entryway (right).

Restructured spaces

The entryway is a transition between the first and second cube. The austere half-light creates an instant sense of peace as you enter. The kitchen and dining room in the first cube were not altered, but the lacquer theme was adopted for the guest room, to increase the sense of continuity.

The second cube contains the large dining room leading to the terrace. It's fairly minimalist, with horizontal strips of white oak on the walls, inspired by the Scandinavian design of the 1960s. This dining room is a major feature, a gallery and hallway, where the owners can admire their artwork, read, or listen to music in a peaceful ambiance.

The large staircase leading to the upper floor, the last cube, was moved to free up the wall, which created an important visual element, as it is another connecting piece. It now leads to the master bedroom. This process of opening up, along with the rearrangement of the spaces, the selection of materials, and the built-in furniture by YH2, creates an overall sense of lightness, in which the decorative object also holds a place of honor.

According to Loukas Yiacouvakis, the counter running alongside the staircase sums up the entirety of this exciting project: the wood and glass structure repeats, on a smaller scale, the theme of fitted cubes that underlies Habitat's offbeat design. "This counter is a wonderfully civilized place for an intimate tête-à-tête," adds the owner.

A MACHINE FOR LIVING

*"Even today, thirty years after Expo, it's hard to find anyone
who visited the fair in 1967 and didn't keep this document."*

Yves Jasmin, talking about the passport given to visitors

*Habitat 67, viewed
from the port of
Montreal. Initially,
these prefabricated
units formed 176
homes (preceding
pages). Nothing
interferes with the
light or the view in
Louis Pauzé's office
in Habitat (above).*

Louis Pauzé sometimes gets the unpleasant feeling that Habitat is just a dream and that once he wakes up, his haven will evaporate. He can't imagine living anywhere else. Indeed, he has been obsessed with Habitat 67 since he was thirteen years old, the year of the World's Fair. Incidentally, Louis has also kept the small passport he received when visiting Expo.

When he would go for walks with his grandfather, the vision of this daring architecture "literally stopped me in my tracks." Thirty-seven years later, he now savors the reality of his dream. During the celebrations of Habitat 67's thirty-fifth anniversary, he was finally able fully to express his gratitude to architect Moshe Safdie in person.

The apartment he's been renting for two years, on the top floor in the southeast section of the complex, is well hidden from view. From the terrace, the landscape unfolds without a break from the north shore to the south bank of the St. Lawrence River. Louis Pauzé is happy to show us the different views from the outside passageways.

"Here, you experience intensely the slightest change in the weather," he says.

These incessant natural rhythms do not bother Louis Pauzé; indeed, he has integrated them within the interior space, which he wanted to be able to transform at will. The harsh sunlight is softened by diaphanous white curtains, which filter the natural light without masking it. He paid serious attention to the lighting; it is a subtle and esthetic tool that creates an impression of relief with the interior geometry and volumes. The owner is both discreet and exuberant, and he expressed this paradox through the use of contemporary lighting fixtures in the living room, along with a system of multicolored spotlights. The pure lines of the Italian furniture (the sofas and tables come from his shop, Bonaldo), and the 1960s oranges and blues add a distinct touch of individuality and spontaneity to the much more formal architecture.

A laboratory of ideas

"Beauty is not enough," insists the fashionable design retailer as he discusses his interior decoration. He needs to be able to set aside his hectic professional life the minute he gets home. People sometimes ask him what he ever does with his

Louis Pauzé opted for a designer look for his Habitat 67 apartment, yet it is lively and multifunctional. The living room and dining room tables are great for either an intimate dinner for two or a large gathering. Transparency and decorative rigor form a contrasting effect in the bedroom (below).

weekends, but he doesn't feel any need to leave his apartment when he has this whole world at his fingertips.

Louis Pauzé's apartment explores light and the infinite possibilities offered by the views outside. The kitchen has not been changed. It is as fresh and as functional as ever, with the original khaki and yellow laminate. The addition of a glass shelf in front of a lovely window has created a new and utilitarian observation site. A small Plexiglas table on the upper floor draws the eye to the landscape stretching to the south.

Mirrors echo the light. Installed in strategic spots in the living room, the stairwell and the bedroom, they appear where you least expect to find them. One, for example, is concealed in the bedroom, which has subtle bright highlights, and it captures the sunlight to illuminate the bed and the room.

All in all, the decoration looks to us like an enigma created by the occupant—and the clues are provided by the objects, like the freshly cut flowers, the rugged and sensual Corno, the astrolabe with its dependable mechanics, and even the toy, a replica from the incredible adventures of Tintin.

AN OASIS IN THE HEART
OF THE LAURENTIAN FOREST

"The scents of the forests that surround me.
Trees dozing in the calm of the evening."

Félix-Antoine Savard

The simple little bridge, constructed by owner Jean-Eudes Desmeules, leads to the cabin (facing page). The autumn bouquet inside expresses all the flamboyance of the Laurentians (above).

The last rays of the sun fade into the night. Within the Desmeules family cabin, the fire burning in the hearth signals the start of an autumn evening, enlivened by improbable stories and children's laughter. Everyone drags his or her bed closer to the warmth of the fire and listens attentively.

"In the middle of a stormy night," starts the interior designer Jean-Eudes Desmeules, "my wife, our three children, and myself were suddenly awakened by what seemed to be strong blows on the door behind the house. I got up and aimed the flashlight out the window into the darkness, but there wasn't anyone there. The noise started up again as soon as I turned my back. I returned to the door and this time shone the beam from my flashlight toward the bottom of the window, and to my amazement, I saw an enormous jackrabbit gnawing on the outside of the wooden door." The marauding creature disappeared, though not without leaving a trace of his brief passage. The deep gashes had to be covered with a metal plate.

This is the stuff that creates the fabric of life within this remote cabin in the woods.

Visual harmony

We reach the refuge via an old road once used by logging trucks, although enormous boulders now conceal the entrance.

The cabin is in the Laurentian Mountains, a one-hour drive from Montreal. It stands like a fortress perched atop an outcrop, at one with the surrounding eighteen-acre (seven-hectare) forest. Two bollards picked up from a shipyard stand guard in front of the main door. "The cabin shields us from the stress of modern life," explains Jean-Eudes Desmeules. "We have lived here winter and summer for twenty-two years, without electricity or running water. Lanterns and the fireplace illuminate our conversations and games with the children. The rainwater we capture is enough for all our needs."

Desmeules was born in Chicoutimi in the Saguenay region and spent his childhood building tree houses. He loves the city, but believes that nature is a treasure to be preserved. As he built, he therefore minimized the impact on the environment: "Only a few trees were cut down to make room for our country house, and

A fir trunk supports the main beam—which is more than forty-three feet (thirteen meters) long—in the central room of this Laurentian house. The visible beam structure and the unique design of the hearth add to the authenticity of the residence (left). The nearby guesthouse, made of cedar logs and mortar, is heated and can accommodate four people. The roof will soon be covered with peat and planted with wild flowers (right).

they were reused in its construction." The semicircular building was constructed using mortar and cedar logs cut from electricity poles, in keeping with the techniques of the so-called Poor Man's Architecture. The logs were lashed and then secured by cement and load-bearing insulation. Almost all the materials used were salvaged from other sites.

This type of architecture, which also exists in Bavaria, seems to bring the forest inside, as reflected in the type of materials used: spruce, pine, and fir. You can smell and touch the forest in every room of the house.

Around the fire

The everyday life of the residents revolves around the large living room, where the fireplace is the central feature. The simple decor is punctuated with a few whimsical touches: pine-tree trunks sharpened like pencils conceal the curtains that close off the three bedrooms and break up the linearity of the walls. This modest wall also ensures privacy.

Desmeules opted for curtains rather than doors in memory of his childhood years in his father's home and also for practical reasons: during the coldest months, the Desmeules move their beds closer to the fire. "The fireplace is a symbolic well around which we still gather to drink," he concludes with a smile. The fireplace-well rests on a steel plate covered with a granite "patchwork" motif. The stones come from the fields around the house, while the blacksmith's hood over the fireplace was picked up at the flea market.

The rustic furniture and a few recycled objects illustrate the owner's tastes, based on the ingrained value of useful and essential things. Basic lights for illumination, an old table for meals, rocking chairs to tell stories, and beds for sleeping. The latter are covered with woven cloth—to which Jean-Eudes Desmeules is stubbornly attached—that were donated by his mother. The imposing wood chest, once his own childhood bed, is now used to store bedcovers.

To fully enjoy the incomparable view, Jean-Eudes Desmeules extended the family fief by adding an outside walk and dug a pond below, which is fed from the river via an ingenious hydraulics system. Even though a few modern conveniences were installed three years ago, they are limited to a few buried electrical lines and cleverly concealed plugs. There is no television and no telephone. And cell phones don't work here, as there's no reception.

The dream carries on, as nothing interferes with the calm, unless it's the omnipresent magic—or the hardworking beaver that tries, unsuccessfully, to dam up the pond every spring.

CONTEMPORARY SPACES
IN OLD MONTREAL

"Here, finally, is the city that we see wedged between the river and the hillside."

Jean Basile

For the apartment in Old Montreal, Daniel Brisset decided to create contrasting ambiances. The curved walls and glass textures in the bathroom brighten up the more austere furnishings (above). The frosted glass on the closet behind the bed captures and reflects a soft light (facing page).

The site is bathed in natural light and the view is nothing short of breathtaking. The loft-style apartment, on the top floor of a residential building in what was once an industrial sector, was created by the well-known interior designer Daniel Brisset for two health professionals. It offers a rare panorama of the Montreal skyline: the downtown area to the north; Pont Jacques Cartier to the east; and part of the Old Port, the St. Lawrence River, and the Lachine Canal walk to the south.

A graduate of Montreal's École des Beaux-Arts, Daniel Brisset is best known for the classical elegance of his work. But he insists on the fact that, above all, spaces must be in perfect harmony with their environment. No "authenticating" detail was left to chance, either in the meticulous lighting plan or in the volumes and layout of the space. The result is a dynamic design that works within the existing structures and visible architectural elements that are characteristic of the industrial site.

Wide open spaces

The entry door leads to a small room that reveals nothing of what awaits on the upper floor. At the top of a beautiful staircase, the interior decor is a skillful blend of urban rhythms and large open space.

The area set aside for communal life is spare and serene, despite the many different functions related to the kitchen, the dining room, the breakfast nook, and reading corner. It features straight lines, perfect angles, high ceilings, and windows everywhere. The lack of curtains or limiting partition walls comes as no surprise. The owners far prefer the views of the Montreal landscape. "We are extremely active and avid travelers. We are in tune with the world around us and we want to see what it has to offer," says one of the owners. Furthermore, the black frames around the inside of the windows help to efface the visual barrier at night. And the floor covering extends from the inside to the terrace, merging the interior and exterior boundaries.

The terrace outside has been designed and furnished with care, as it is an essential element in the well-being of the inhabitants. Satisfied with the rooftop view of Montreal, we turn back toward the living room. It now becomes clear that the concrete columns as well as the room lighting are elegant reinterpretatations of a

The darker colors of the kitchen do not dampen the luminosity of the living room (left). The eating nook with a view over the Montreal rooftops combines the natural simplicity of wood with reproductions of the Series 7 chair by Arne Jacobsen.

monumental landmark nearby: grain silo number 5, which the famous architect Le Corbusier admired.

Giving substance to form and texture

Designed as a blend of intimacy and openness, the apartment radiates warmth and friendliness. "I like the old as much as the modern, bright colors as well as matching colors, theatrical decors as well as intimate spaces," says Daniel Brisset. But here, everything is in a contemporary mode.

The designer carefully selected rugged and refined materials and varied textures. The Wassily chairs, which are simple wood, suede, and fur pieces, create rich textures that are in harmony with the fluidity of the concrete and steel, Chinese slate, and warm tones. The kitchen, the heart of the house, is a working area open to all and designed with efficiency in mind. Daniel Brisset concealed the utilitarian aspects to avoid creating visual obstacles.

The theme of openness is repeated in the bedroom. The designer did not install a door so as to not break the movement and light: crackled glass suffices to identify the sleeping area, which leads to the bathroom. Here, the angular design is replaced by sensual curves and luminous Caribbean blue and mandarin orange colors.

Old Montreal has seen a revival in the last decade. It combines the effervescence of urban life—galleries, shops, and cafés—with outdoor activities. "This apartment fulfills our urban sides. Plus, it's exactly eighty-seven miles (one hundred and forty kilometers) from our summer house in the south and exactly eighty-seven miles (one hundred and forty kilometers) from our winter residence in the north. It is the focal point of our current existence," conclude the owners.

GRAPHIC DESIGN AND COLOR IN HABITAT 67

"Daylight, summoned for the second time, came into its own like a large spectacular poppy on its stem."

Anne Hébert

Most terraces in Habitat 67 are fairly monochromatic; the touch of color here is a cheerful addition (above). The bedroom features a sober style, though with a whimsical touch provided by the swing mirror on wheels (facing page).

In 2001, the Morins left their old home in the Notre-Dame-de-Grâce district of Montreal and moved to Habitat 67. They remodeled the lively contemporary space themselves, a bold composition in the image of their agency, Republik, and of themselves. In short, to quote Dominique Morin, "The space combines our profession as graphic designers and our love of design."

The cold concrete architecture vanishes under the exuberance of the pure 1960s ambiance, which makes sense for a kitchen and living room humming with activity. The lifestyle of the occupants is visible in the small gestures of everyday life, yand is also revealed in this atmosphere of gourmet dining.

The narrow walls were removed from the kitchen laboratory, which is now the major hub of the apartment, opposite the living room, much to the delight of the hosts and their guests. In Quebec, the kitchen is a place where everyone gathers, especially while meals are being prepared. The magenta color on the walls selected by Dominique Morin is another highlight, inspired by the shade of the tulip chairs. "When I come home, I like to contemplate this wall. Plus, the full-length windows make me feel like I'm outside," she says. The light and intelligent touch used here is revealed in several features.

Humor and fluidity

Designer Daniel Morin's views on decoration are clear: "It's not about adding, but about taking away." The spaces are not large; no objects are out of context in the tightly designed concept. He adds: "There is no improvisation, everything was selected in terms of color, shape, and style." When they moved in, it was difficult to select works from their large collection, says Dominique Morin. But the survivors, including a Riopelle, highlight this sober yet dazzling world that feels like a vacation home.

The objects that demonstrate "humor without caricature," such as the yellow coffeemaker and the orange telephone in the kitchen, designate the kitchen and contrast with the serious geometry of the stainless steel blocks. The terrace, on the other hand (Daniel Morin's favorite spot), is decorated in translucent materials for a calm visual experience. "I spend a lot a time here, especially in the summer. From here, I can see the wide landscape as well as the small bits of my space: the living

The architectural rigor of Habitat 67 has disappeared in this brightly colored apartment. The entryway leads to the kitchen, a three-dimensional graphic design in itself that places as much importance on color and shape as on treasured objects (right). In the living room, the raw power of the triptych on wood by Montreal artist Michelle Assal adds character to the contemporary design (left).

room, our bedroom, the bathroom," says Daniel Morin. There is something magical about peeking into someone's private space for a few minutes, even if as in this case, it's your own. This magic is also present in the logical progression of the decorative theme.

The narrow corridor that was to have been painted orange remained white. To furnish it, Daniel Morin made a series of bundles of wood and placed them in a line, creating the impression of a small grove: "I don't want an ambiance that is in conflict with reality. We live in a northern country, we have snow, cold, and bare trees that nonetheless provide heat."

The serenity of the corridor precedes the privacy of the bathroom and the two bedrooms. Their son's is brightly colored, while theirs is bathed in light and transparency. This minimalism is enhanced by the choice of furniture, preferably white, gray, or brown. "All our windows are bare so that we can enjoy this beautiful light," notes Dominique Morin, though they do protect their privacy and that of their neighbors.

"Habitat is a small community where people stay in close touch. There are many opportunities for exchanges," she says. Often groups of architecture students from abroad come to visit the complex. The Morins have hosted such groups twice; they are aware that Habitat is an essential piece of contemporary architecture. They remain open and are happy to contribute to the long life of this unique structure.

THE BUCOLIC CHARM
OF DUNHAVEN

*"I invited her to sit on the kitchen stool while I prepared
the dough for an apple pie—it being the season—and roasted my peppers."*

Jean-Louis Tremblay

*Dunhaven, set amid
nearly seven acres
of greenery in
Magog in the
Eastern Townships,
has remained
faithful to the
region's architecture
and cachet.
The successive
remodelings, the
vegetable garden,
the outdoor pool,
the pavilion, and
the woodwork are
all based on an
appreciation of
nature (above).*

Spencer the griffon does not hunt the ducks in the pond, interior designer Johanne Dunn assures us as we visit the English garden behind the property she and her husband purchased in the town of Magog in 1922. The property—Dunhaven, named in memory of the country house that belonged to the owner's grandfather—is flanked by a garage and a garden pavilion, and is a refuge for its occupants: deer, ducks, and Canada geese.

The remodeling efforts put into this large, vaguely neo-Gothic home don't look as if they were easy. "Our apartment in Montreal is really only a pied-à-terre. We plan to live in Dunhaven for a long time," says Johanne Dunn. The couple constructed the garage, among the many other projects, creating a guest suite on the upper floor; they also redesigned the layout, and added and moved rooms. The new addition includes the current kitchen and main bedroom, while the former kitchen was transformed into a dining room. These large interior spaces have clearly served as a creative outlet for the designer's passion for colors and materials. The moldings, woodwork, and profusion of diverse textures and motifs, both on the ground floor and the upper floor, add a touch of relaxed spontaneity. Even the wood is painted: a floral design painted on the living room floor matches the furniture fabric, a decorative solution that is repeated in the dining room. A fondness for bright colors is also evident in a clear preference for cherry red.

Not only do we want to linger, we want to touch everything. Windows, walls, sofas, and tables all have an animal theme. This bucolic ambiance is fully in keeping with the spirit of the Eastern Townships; spare, neutral interiors just wouldn't fit in here. Although comfort is a priority for the Dunns, there is plenty of room for collectors' items and a few period furniture pieces, all family heirlooms. A plush armchair by the fire presents an irresistible invitation to sip a glass of wine before dinner.

The kitchen is the designer's uncontested domain. "We eat almost every meal here. Friends like to be here, too," says Johanne Dunn. She has recreated a welcoming room with Provencal touches. The two-tone surface treatment, and the choice of decorative and architectural elements, makes this a perfect place to share the delights of a meal. In the designer's opinion, naming a house is a very important moment, as it personalizes it. Dunhaven radiates joie de vivre, as do all its residents.

Tea is served in the living room of a Victorian home in the Eastern Townships. This cozy room is a study in heterogeneous styles: a mountain goat's head overlooks the fine porcelain and elegant rug. The head is in keeping with Johanne Dunn's favorite animal theme (left). The decoration in the dining room combines brilliant yellows and reds with cotton prints and gingham (top right). The floor of this room is adorned with an image of the four seasons (bottom right).

A HOUSE ON THE ÎLES DE LA MADELEINE

"The girls resist the swirls
swing from the unending moorings where all thirsts are quenched
nudity lives in the heart of the land like a word"
Anne Peyrouse

A small stove stands guard in the center of this Îles de la Madeleine home (above). The materials create a harmonious link between the diverse living areas (right).

A pretty yellow house with a red roof stands alone facing the immensity of the sea. It looks peaceful, yet its history is anything but, as we discover from the owners. This professional couple runs a health information website. They had lived in Montreal for several years and for some time had wanted to purchase property on the Îles de la Madeleine.

"We were visiting friends in Bassin [a village on the Île du Havre Aubert], when we bought a parish hall on the spur of the moment," explains the owner, who was born on the magnificent archipelago. The building, located in front of Bassin's church, was constructed in the 1930s. It didn't have any land or even an interesting view, but they liked the architecture. The large structure was divided in two so that they could move it more easily to an immense plot of land just under a mile outside the village. Moving a home on the islands is not an unusual event, possibly less so than in any other part of Quebec.

The owners hired a young architect, Johanne Béland. "When we first met, in 1998, they showed me a number of books. One of them depicted the home of Pablo Neruda in Chile. I could easily see these people living in this type of a house, filled with treasures from the sea," remembers the architect.

The house faces directly south and gets tremendous of sunlight. Certain elements were preserved, such as the bell tower and the windows facing the road, as well as the stage inside the house, which was once used for performances and film projections.

We are struck by the immense interior, which consists of the living area, the kitchen, and the dining room. The preference for wood, particularly pine and ash, adds to the warmth of this environment designed around a love of nature. The architect successfully created "small, intimate spaces enclosed within larger ones" through the use of diverse materials, placement of furniture, interplay of levels between the veranda and the dining room, and a multipurpose piece of furniture at the entrance, which acts as a partition. It serves as a closet, wardrobe, or credenza, depending on the room it faces. This piece of furniture was necessary to balance the entryway. A wide corridor leads to the four bedrooms, the bathroom, and the owner's study. Right above it, the mezzanine includes a workspace, a small sitting room,

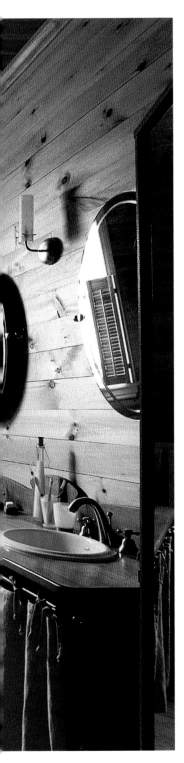

and a private bathroom. It also leads to the bell tower, "a terrific place to sulk," says the daughter of the couple, who was there on a visit.

Blending in with the landscape

The curved line echoes the natural lines of the sea and the coast. "I appreciate straight lines, but I think it was essential to link this house to the landscape," explains Johanne Béland. The house is furnished and decorated simply, and the natural materials were selected for their discretion. "I prefer pure lines. I find that my thoughts are scattered in a cluttered environment," notes the owner, who designed the interiors. The transition from one room to another is harmonious, and everything is directed toward enhancing both physical and spiritual well-being. The dominant colors mirror those of the landscape outside, like the wildflowers and light green of the fields. The owner opted for a "peaceful sea" blue for her husband's study. "I am more active than contemplative. But this blue is soothing, and my work has to be organized in a calm space," he says.

The functional kitchen also reflects the quest for comfort. The architect wanted to create an older, more antique look, through the use of forms, surfaces, and woodwork. She designed the work surface as a table, an object symbolizing the owner's pleasure in cooking and entertaining. Each area has been reinterpreted in terms of comfort: the veranda is relatively spartan, as a place of reflection, while the more elegant living room features soft colors and motifs that foster intimate conversations among friends.

Choosing an object is never a neutral decision. The owners wanted each object to have a meaning: two masks against a wall representing a stylized sun remind them of their two children, who work with the Cirque du Soleil. Much of the artwork deals with the theme of transparency and history: among others, fascinating objects in blown glass, paintings, and a magnificent collection of photographs of the region. The owners also found old film posters that they have had framed. They feel that this is a way of preserving history.

This concern with maintaining a certain continuity through architecture has revived the past. From the new semicircular window in the bell tower, you can now see the building that used to be house's neighbor—the church of Bassin.

The serene bedroom lets in the calm light of the Îles de la Madeleine. The residents especially love the winter sunrises (above). The natural décor of the bathroom sets off the antique cast-iron bathtub (left).

A VICTORIAN HOME
IN MONTREAL

*"What do the old streets
of old cities tell you?"*
Émile Nelligan

*Like many
Victorian
residences, this
house in Montreal
still has its original
glass panels
(above).*

Square Saint-Louis is not only located in one of Montreal's trendy neighborhoods, the Plateau, it also has a unique architectural heritage. Constructed in 1876, and well known as the favorite promenade of one of its famous residents, the Québécois poet Émile Nelligan, the square is a priceless visual attraction for everyone who passes through. Cornices, wood or tinplate pediments, friezes, columns, and colorful capitals showcase the austere limestone façades of the late-nineteenth-century bourgeois homes. A Victorian home awaits us farther to the north on Rue Laval. It belonged to merchants and was later a boarding house. For the last twenty-five years, it has been the private residence of a couple of television producers. This house echoes the love of eclecticism that characterized the Victorian period.

The couple's professional and family life is intense, and they required a serene environment where they could recharge their batteries. Over time, the rooms were refurnished with objects picked up at flea markets and during travels abroad. "This house is a good reflection of us as we only put what we love in it—and if we like an object, my husband and I always find a place for it," says the owner.

The decorative object is something of a treasure, while the combination of classic and contemporary architecture creates the backdrop. The couple met Serge Lafrance in 1997, which proved decisive, as their great passion for primitive objects and bright colors resonated with the interior designer. "My goal was to modernize this Victorian house, while preserving its original feeling and period character," explains Serge Lafrance. He therefore favored deep greens and luminous yellows, while adding a more convivial lighting system. He also significantly redesigned the dining room and kitchen on the ground floor, so that the owners' diverse styles remained coherent.

The designer added an elegant touch to the small room that serves as a study on the upper floor. His improvised diaphanous draped fabric and cherry wood and mahogany desk fit perfectly into this contrasting and theatrical decor. What does this old house have to tell? It sometimes transmits the fleeting charm of past lives, but above all, it reflects a very contemporary lifestyle based on simple shapes and textures.

The soft patina of the wood in the dining room of this Victorian Montreal home has been combined with rough brick. The small glass shelves on the wall, created by the owners and designers, showcase a collection of terra-cotta works from South and Central America. On the wall to the right is a superb retablo *(with a frame made of corn paste)* by Peruvian artist Nicario Jiménez *(left)*. The fireplace decorated with the original floral motif tiles warms up the small living room *(top right)*. The immaculate upstairs bathroom forms a lovely backdrop *(bottom right)*.

THE TOWER HOUSE

*"My best moments in recent years have probably been spent on the terrace,
a glass in my hand, watching my friend in the distance walking through my garden."*

Stéphane Bourguignon

W̲e are in Little Italy, a dense, cosmopolitan neighborhood where picturesque staircases set off the disparate architectural styles. Most of the residential buildings are constructed in tight rows, with backyards stretching behind as far as the back alley—the favorite playground for the children of Montreal. It's a neighborhood of *dépanneurs**, cafés, and restaurants.

"Living in the city for us means having the freedom to move," says Marie-Claude Hamelin. "It also means living peacefully in a private place facing a garden."

In 2000, the architects purchased a bungalow and a garage for almost nothing. There was nothing worth saving, except perhaps the courtyard and its old tree. "We didn't really come into the project with an idea, but we were inspired by the environment," explains the architect. Their plans took shape as they walked around, studying the shape of buildings and becoming familiar with the rhythms of daily life in the neighborhood.

The three-floor house has a façade inspired by Italian rationalism. The yellow brick structure, with a balcony on the upper floor, seems to echo the style of the school across the street. The decision to use corten* steel for the balcony and entryway may be somewhat disconcerting, but it gives the recent building something of a lived-in look. The tower house is protected from people looking in from the street, as the opaque windows on the ground floor shield the interior.

The urban countryside

The diffuse light creates a more intimate ambiance inside the tower house in Montreal (above). The mezzanine facing the garden is designed for rest and play (facing page).

The symmetrical spaces inside are arranged in a logical hierarchy. The communal "zone" on the ground floor includes the kitchen and the dining room. It was designed to maximize the living space; all the utilitarian equipment is concealed behind panels and in the central island, which is the command central station for activities inside and out. The garage door is an essential element, as soon becomes clear: once it's raised, the room, which was already airy, suddenly opens out into the garden. This door is rarely closed in the summer, and every meal always includes the deck.

There's something exotic about the overall design. Marie-Claude Hamelin explains, "We had just returned from a trip to Vietnam. It's possible that our decision to put in a lacquered, coffered ceiling and a floor covering inside similar to

The kitchen in the tower house illustrates the contrast of textures and opaque surfaces. The garage door blurs the traditional concept of indoors and outdoors (left). Minimalism also extends to the deck the enclosed garden, a haven in the heart of Montreal.

the one on the outside deck comes from that trip." The rich texture of the wood and the surfaces constitutes the decorative feature in this pared-down architecture.

The staircase leads to the second zone, marking the climb to the sacrosanct private areas. The living room on the mezzanine, which runs along three walls, is characterized by simplicity and comfort. One flight up, the top floor includes two bedrooms and a bathroom. The master bedroom is a wonderful place to relax, as well as to watch the urban landscape. As for the children, they have a view over the garden.

The tower house is just a few minutes from the flower stalls and vegetable stands of the marché Jean Talon. The solitary tree adds to the country feel and forms a symbolic buffer between the residents and the city. Since 1994, YH2 has designed a number of original contemporary projects, notably an apartment at Habitat 67; the summer residence on the Îles de la Madeleine, which belongs to their Habitat client; and the interior design for the Hôtel Gault in Montreal. The tower house, which they remodeled in 2002, is a fascinating residence, garden, and studio design. This style of architecture has resulted in a new perception of space, and for the child of the house, the concept of "outside" now means everything that's beyond the other side of the enclosed garden.

A LOFT IN A FORMER WAREHOUSE

"I remember the lavish receptions held in the commander's house.
Squeezed into our tight red uniforms, our hands gloved in white, we solemnly entered the immense dining room,
to the slow rhythm of a military march."

One of Stéphane Allard's memories from the Royal Military College in Kingston, Ontario, where he was an assistant squadron leader.

The designer Serge Lafrance used a fluid, contemporary design in the kitchen to offset the overall classicism of this loft in Old Montreal. The brightly lit study in red and black includes a functional work surface, which also doubles as a side table and eating area (above).

The many years spent at the military college left a strong impression on Stéphane Allard, and he remained deeply attached to conventions. Located in a restored former warehouse named "La Caserne," in Old Montreal, this magnificent loft would give anyone a sense of permanence. We discover with pleasure the owner's desire to recreate the sumptuous officers' mess at the Royal Military College.

His memories have remained perfectly clear, indeed, sharpened by a passion for beautiful objects and antique furniture. At home, Stéphane Allard momentarily forgets his responsibilities as head of a company specializing in the production of laboratory equipment used in ballistics. "I have always avoided following trends. I prefer the stability of the classical style," he explains. Paradoxically, he put his home into the hands of Serge Lafrance, who tends to favor contemporary design over classicism. Stéphane Allard does not regret his decision: "Serge taught me a great deal about decoration and its possibilities."

A harmonious symphony of styles

Everything fits together naturally in this apartment, although it is furnished with different and elaborately ornamented styles. Stéphane Allard is rigorous in arranging these styles, which include Directory and Queen Anne, among others. The design inherent in these two styles seems to illustrate the political regimes that shaped Quebec to the present day. But let's leave behind military conquests to concentrate on the designer's strategies for remodeling, which resulted in a series of interventions aimed at reviving the rooms that seemed impervious to the architectural beauty of the spot.

"It was essential to give this loft its own character, in other words, to create well-lit and spacious areas that set off the interesting architectural elements that were already here," explains Serge Lafrance. The designer opted for the luminosity of yellow, in order to compensate for the light absorbed by the brick walls and wood furniture. He also added directional lighting systems, with which the owner can create contrasting areas of light and shadow.

This Old Montreal loft features historical references and an intimate ambiance, with an Empire dining room table and Biedermeier chairs alongside the rough masonry walls (left). The bedroom is more sober: above the Mission-style bed, designed by the owner, is a copy of a painting by Tamara De Lempicka, also by the owner (below).

Once the partition walls were removed, the apartment offered a lovely view of the luxury room in the back. For example, a tiny bedroom by the entrance was transformed into a large vestibule with a view of the magnificent windows curtained in black and of the kitchen, the nerve center of all activity. Classicism gave way to the modernity and functionality imagined by the designer. The kitchen, designed by the architect Jean Raymond, one of Serge Lafrance's collaborators, is the hub for frequent dinner parties. It is perfectly integrated into the overall design.

The underlying architectural structure and the layout of living spaces can be used in different ways: the music corner is good for relaxing and pre-dinner drinks, while the "select club" room is conducive to enjoying a cigar in front of the fireplace after a good dinner. The elegant bedroom, in tones of sage and varnished wood, is a fitting end to the evening. For Stéphane Allard, each object is a conquest that involves more than the patina of the past; they are interlinked by a specific context or emotion. An enthusiastic and faithful collector, Stéphane Allard will keep the books, decorative objects, furniture, as well as his own canvases, for a very long time.

THE ART OF SALVAGE
IN A FORMER SCHOOL

*"As I turned my head just to see if the river would appear for an instant,
I saw an apparition appear suddenly between two gray strips, I couldn't tell if it was near or far."*

Christiane Duchesne

The wooden banister has been bleached by the sun; it adds relief to the house on the Gaspé Peninsula (above). A counter from a general store creates an unusual work surface in the kitchen (facing page).

Martin Gagnon and his partner and associate Jean-Luc Leblond both love to salvage materials and objects from old buildings. The housing company in Bic, in the Lower St. Lawrence, illustrates this talent of reinterpreting raw materials and objects. In 2001, they moved into the former school of Métis-sur-Mer (in the Les Boules region) that was constructed in 1903. "We had always dreamed of having a summer home here. The former owner was reluctant to give up the building, but he understood that we would preserve its history and architecture," explains Martin Gagnon. Everything that came their way was a treasure, and the school soon became a magnificent haven for many "shipwrecked survivors": driftwood, stones, and old objects.

It's impossible to resist the charm of this structure, with its roof and six dormer windows. Everything was preserved intact, with the exception of the enclosed porch, which was transformed into an open veranda. The door leads to a high-ceilinged vestibule; we wouldn't be surprised to see a cluster of schoolchildren rushing into the entrance.

The residents opted for simplicity and created a series of large, sunny spaces. From the entryway, we move into the dining room, one of the former classrooms. The west wall leads to the outside. The house has two wood stoves, which create a warm ambiance. In the dining room, the residents created a base of stones for one of the stoves. The overall effect, combined with the slightly kitsch furniture and red and yellow accessories, demonstrates the owners' taste for the picturesque. "We are eternal scavengers," says Martin Gagnon.

Salvaging is the key principle

The owners instantly acknowledge the importance of the kitchen. "We make all our major decisions here," explains Martin Gagnon. The love affair with natural light continues in this room, where windows fill up the entire east wall of the dining room. In addition, these rooms have a view of the pretty deck and the vast stretch of river.

Recycling has its own vocabulary; adapting an object so that it serves a purpose other than what it was designed for gives it a much richer dimension. Above the

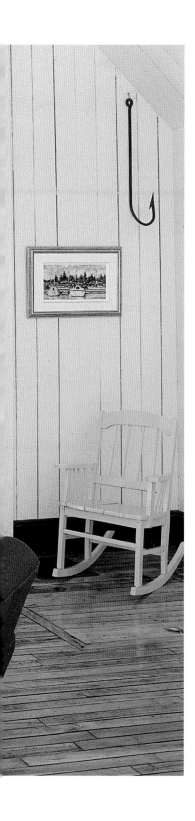

The living room of this Gaspé Peninsula home features the silent poetry of objects. The ships' beacons keep a storm watch, while an old armchair and small yellow rocking chair create a cozy atmosphere. An old wooden boat from the 1920s has been transformed into a bookshelf.

dining room table, for example, a model wooden ship and an old plank form an unusual suspended light fixture.

We climb upstairs, noting the driftwood used as a banister. An old armchair on the landing presents an inviting place to rest. Other treasures await in the five bedrooms, and it is touching to see the geometry homework decorating the walls of the children's room.

The bathroom takes us suddenly to another world, that of luxury and contemporary design. Living in an environment of endlessly wide landscapes is also a luxury. According to Martin Gagnon: "Everything is excessive here, and we could no longer live in a small space. We have to be able to breathe and see the beauty of nature directly." The country-style landscaping, designed to preserve the authentic character of the property, uses plants common in the region, notably wild roses.

As summer draws to a close, the residents prepare to close up their homes, a ritual that is always a nostalgic moment for everyone. They're ready to come back, even before they've left.

A FORMER FUR WAREHOUSE
OCCUPIED BY A FRENCHMAN

*"There was also the pungent smoke from late cooking fires rising from a few chimneys. Here and there, the odor of
pastries or chickens cooking was still wafting out of the openings cut into the sides of the houses."*

Gaétan Leboeuf

*This former
Montreal
warehouse still
has its original
windows.*

Christophe Nouaille's life is filled with the fragrance of lovingly prepared dishes. It matters little where the grandson of Marie-Antoinette Cartet, owner of the famous Parisian restaurant Le Cartet, decides to live, as his world will always revolve around culinary pleasures.

He arrived in Montreal in 1992 with a single bag containing all his worldy belongings. Christophe Nouaille soon made his entry into the movies—as a caterer to the Montreal film community. In 1999, with his partner and associate Denis Bubois, he acquired a building located at the western edge of Old Montreal, in a dynamic neighborhood with thriving businesses and many residential buildings. The former fur warehouse at 106 rue McGill dates to 1889 and was built by the legendary Hudson's Bay Company. Novaille turned it into the popular food shop Le Cartet.

The owners live above the shop. A door in the back of the shop leads to a long staircase that climbs to the dining room, where the familiar smell of strawberry jam still floats in the air. The decor is decidedly simple, with brick walls painted white and old wood floors. Yet it's very cozy. The lovely outside terrace and the adjoining professional kitchen, both set off by natural light, pine, and glass, add to the ambiance.

During the summer, the terrace is filled with flowers that compete with the theatrical kitchen that is large enough for all the friends who come by. Christophe Nouaille notes: "Everyone participates in preparing the meals, as soon as all the guests arrive." In the winter, when the garden is frozen over, everyone gathers around the table or the counter in the dining room.

Form follows function

"Our efforts can be summed up as meeting the client's needs through architectural elements rather than decorative ones," says architect Stéphane Pratte of Atelier in situ. The open arches and original columns, painted white, along with the furniture, create fluidity and space in the overall layout. The shapes and materials, like metal and leather, decorate these living areas in a simple way, and as with food the simplest ingredients are often the best. The heavy fire door salvaged by

The combination of a contemporary chair and an anachronistic tree-trunk chair is surprising in the dining room of this former Montreal fur warehouse. This room also has other references: the geometric "love" work, and spaghetti painted in matching tones (left). The fresh design of the bedroom extends to the sea-blue bathroom (below).

the architects creates an immediate break. Just behind it is the bedroom and open bathroom, with a shower space in between that creates a transition area toward the privacy of the bedroom.

The owners would rather live in the space than furnish it. "We don't need much, and each object has to have a practical purpose," says Christophe Nouaille. The decoration is nonetheless contemporary, with a preference for clean lines and basic shapes—although the occasional antique piece can be found amongst the minimal modernity. The owner's detachment in terms of objects is also clear in the way they occupy their space. They often allow film crews to work here; this loft could one day become a public space devoted to the arts of the table, among other activities.

Is it any surprise to discover that Christophe Nouaille keeps his most precious possession in the kitchen? It was given to him by his grandmother Marie-Antoinette: an old recipe book called *L'Art culinaire moderne* by Henri-Paul Pellaprat, the reference work she used when she first started her career.

A DREAM HOUSE ON A LAKE
IN LA MAURICIE

"His work must facilitate man's life in the temple, the city, at home, create order and beauty in these places."

Paul-Émile Borduas on the art of the architect

A Bélanger stove from 1910 reigns over the kitchen in the Mauricie villa. It is still prized for its looks and usefulness, notably the plate warmer and the iron ornaments.

D esigning a residence from the bottom up and selecting the materials and volumes requires intense planning and a dream. For the architect Pierre Thibault, a house creates memories drawn from its own personal vocabulary of spatial sensations. In addition to the impressions it provokes, the villa on a Mauricie lake is the film on which the souls of the residents are captured, as well as those of those who participated in its construction: the architect, the interior designer, and the young contractor Réjean Désilets, who oversaw the building project.

For the owners, who live in Montreal—a retired lawyer and his wife—the dream began thirty years ago. "I always wanted to have a simple, untraditional wooden house in the middle of the forest," he explains. "I wanted to take the Quebec residential style a step further." He acquired the property in 1994, and in 1995 shared his vision of architecture with Pierre Thibault. And in 1997, he hired the architect. La Mauricie is a vast territory dotted with lakes and forests, a perfect place to construct what would be a successful project, both as a contemporary architectural design and a building perfectly integrated in its environment.

Metamorphic architecture

Pierre Thibault draws a parallel between the forest and Rome, where he lived in 1998 after winning the Prix de Rome, awarded by the Canada Council. This gave him the opportunity to live in the Italian capital for one year. Whenever he visited La Mauricie, he was amazed to rediscover the same nonchalance in nature that he so loved in Italy. He immersed himself in the places and created sketches on site that he later used for models.

After many visits, throughout one season and another, the client and his architect found a site on the peninsula, with an optimum view of the lake. "But during a subsequent meeting, I decided to start from scratch. We stacked up branches so that we could climb up to see the landscape, but this time, at the level of the future house," says the owner.

The villa unfolds like a series of stage sets. "Walking from one room to another lets you enjoy different perceptions, and get a clearer idea of the spaces," says Pierre Thibault. To the north, the house is hidden from the excesses of modern life by a palisade of vertical gray pine logs. To the south, on the other hand, it offers a

The slightest variations in the winter light, shining through the large windows, are captured in the villa's dining room. The room is furnished simply, so as not to interfere with the view of the forest. There are no curtains, but the windows are equipped with a system of automatic blinds.

The corridor of the villa in La Mauricie is characterized by traditional elements, with, for example, an antique Québécois chair (right). The bathroom is behind the bedroom wall; it is decorated in white marble and the windows offer a breath of fresh air (facing page, top). The simple lighting in the bedroom contributes to the austere ambiance (facing page, bottom).

generous view of the wild natural beauty, with a verandah protected by netting. The "column" trunks, both outside and inside, and the similar wall treatment within and without also blur the reality. The forest house vibrates to the rhythm of the light, wind, colors, and scents of each distinct season.

The interior offers glimpses of bits of sky and treetops from the palisade windows, views of the lake from the living room, and the sight of an island that appears from the kitchen windows—the best lookout point for observing the wildlife. Although it stands within a contemporary Italian design scheme, the gleaming Bélanger stove in the kitchen embodies the importance of entertaining and sharing culinary pleasures so prevalent in Quebec. The owners are excellent cooks and love to share this tradition, much to the pleasure of their guests. During the winter, the stove is also used to heat the room and toast bread on Sunday mornings.

The lake is no longer visible from the eastern side of the villa; the forest stretches out instead. "I love the transitions. In the bedroom, for example, the ceiling is lower, which gives a greater sense of comfort and security," notes the owner. The difference in the roof levels expresses the notion of slipping into nature. The outside surfaces were left untreated and the graying wood is a reminder of passing time.

A harmonious design

The immense fireplace in the living room is the center of the house, the "act of faith" on the part of the owner, who thought it was too excessive. In the winter, protected from the storms, this excess is comforting as it fills the room with heat.

The interior designer René Desjardins worked to capture the abundance of the surrounding landscape, and the natural tones are reminiscent of the color of tree bark. The use of raw materials, such as light-colored slate arranged in a staggered pattern, suggests the unpredictable. He created a sense of fluidity for certain spaces and designed simple lighting to set off the architecture and the artwork. The staircase behind the fireplace leads to the mezzanine and a magnificent mandarin red structure. "I wanted this passageway to have a strong vitality," explains René Desjardins. His design for the library partition leads to the purity and modernity of the study, tucked away in the bosom of the forest. The cohabitation of various furniture styles works harmoniously. There are relatively few objects, as the owner does not want to become a slave to them.

Being in the house feels like walking in the forest. Indeed, according to Pierre Thibault, the two columns in the living room that seem to embrace each other are representative of this communion with nature. The communion is in listening to the slightest movements of the heart and spirit. This keen music lover listens to favorite works almost day and night in Montreal, but avoids them in this house. "Music is an intruder. I prefer the rustling of the leaves and the tumbling water."

The ceiling of the living room in the Mauricie villa rises to a height of over twenty-five feet (eight meters). To achieve its immense size, the tall fireplace was constructed with nearly 33,000 pounds (15,000 kilograms) of stones.

PURE DESIGN
IN A MONTREAL LOFT

*"In truth, the course of a life is chaotic and unpredictable.
No fiction could mask the 'unpredictable' order of existence."*

Hubert Aquin

*Rigor is the
defining concept
for the décor of
the bathing area,
kitchen, and
bedroom in this
Montreal loft
(above and facing
page).*

We find the interior designer Jacques Bilodeau in a rather dreary part of Montreal. The place he's been living for almost three years now is adjacent to the train tracks and a few industrial buildings; both the neighborhood and its appearance are disconcerting. We shouldn't have been surprised to see that this advocate of sheet metal decided to live in a factory that used to manufacture metal. A small children's playground in front reflects the "progressive" residential efforts underway in the neighborhood, a process that is widespread in Montreal.

The rectangle of bricks, painted white, forms an almost solid wall; wide windows along the street create lovely openings, but they are too high up to allow people to see inside. In fact, the building illustrates the creator's concept of a cathedral built for research and development, to quote Jacques Bilodeau, "where the effects of the space on people lead to reflection."

Jacques Bilodeau is, by nature, drawn to the use of steel; this material is also easy to work with, has non-uniform surfaces, and can take on dynamic and much more complex textures. He appreciates the rough aspect of steel, because "when you overwork a project, you lose the initial idea." His favorite materials are steel, stainless steel, plastic, and industrial felt. It has a destabilizing effect on the viewer. According to the designer, "People recognize my process, without having to appropriate its contents."

Movement is an underlying theme in this comfortable loft, which is heated by water flowing in pipes under the concrete slab. "Initially, I wanted to create a transformable living space, which could be totally altered in terms of height and angles," says Jacques Bilodeau, pointing out the sliding horizontal structures that greet the visitor on the ground floor. These structures vary from large dining room tables to conference tables, and a sliding platform that holds changeable sculpture chairs.

The panels separating the main living area from the kitchen are also sliding partitions. Behind these walls, the concept of the laboratory underlying the contemporary kitchen design is pursued in its most literal sense. Jacques Bilodeau's extreme and extraordinarily pared down design is not only somewhat disturbing; his work is also surprising because of his use of recycled or salvaged materials and objects. The stainless steel cabinet in the kitchen comes from a hospital, as does the bath, a perfect cube at the end of the kitchen.

Two staircases lead upstairs. One leads to the bedroom, where Axelle, a six-year-old basset hound, likes to sleep in the dark interior decorated in shades of deep blue, anthracite, and brown. The designer's bedroom has used the movement and the transformation that lies at the heart of his creativity to create an unusual bed: the "table" at the foot of the bed holds a sculptural lighting fixture; it is also a cover that can be moved over the bed.

The other staircase leads to the living room, which is lighted simply with a system of fluorescent rail-mounted fixtures, creating a meditative semi-dark ambiance of black and steel gray. In such a monastic setting, the shower is a purification rite.

"I have no use for technology; I still draw all my plans by hand, but I love technical mechanisms," reveals Jacques Bilodeau. By simply pressing a button, he opens the huge garage door leading to the garden. The "black pearl," as it has been nicknamed by a Montreal magazine, is finally lit up for the outside world.

A COUNTRY HOUSE ON THE ÎLES DE LA MADELEINE

"The desert, still. The dunes are watching me. They are moving, secretly; the ground vibrates under my feet. From the corner of my eye, I make out shapes, the crests and valleys that form and dissolve."

Guillaume Vigneault

The property on the Îles de la Madeleine has a surprising layout. It is faced with cedar planks painted a light blue, and the passageway is made of natural-colored cedar planks (above). In keeping with the seaside location, the railing on the mezzanine was created with steel wire ropes (facing page).

Perched high on a hill on the Île de Havre aux Maisons, we catch sight of our destination below: two violet blue spots surrounded by greenery. The architectural complex corresponds to the vocabulary of the Îles de la Madeleine: the main house and its shop are placed haphazardly in relation to nearby buildings. Yet the overall effect is troubling. It's because Marie-Claude Hamelin and Loukas Yiacouvakis (YH2) have designed a unique country house for their Montreal clients. "We wanted to give it the candor of a child's drawing, make it as naive as the landscape of the islands," explains Loukas Yiacouvakis.

Given the initial project—which involved renovating and enlarging the existing house—the architects decided to construct a second building, linked to the main house by a raised passageway. "From a simple renovation project, we moved on to an overall architectural plan, which would be a normal yet destabilizing design, what Roland Barthes called 'a worrisome strangeness.'" But the house itself is not disturbing; it is the angularity that catches your attention. The buildings seem to be playing hide-and-seek, depending on the place from which you view them. They also radiate an architectural well-being that feels like vacation.

"We also wanted this house to be reconnected to the ground, as its major fault came from the fact that the existing structure was entirely off the ground, perched on foundations six feet [two meters] high," continues the architect. The main building was totally transformed and is now fully integrated into its new landscaped surroundings. The deck rests on a grassy knoll ringed by stones. Large windows maintain a new and open relationship between the inside and the outside.

Whimsical interior

The building is a former schoolhouse, transported here from another village. It became a barn and was placed here, on its current foundation. Later, other renovations transformed it into a private residence, which the couple then purchased; After visiting the attic, the architects discovered such a beautiful framed roof structure that they decided to uncover it. According to Loukas Yiacouvakis, it is a return to basics, to the structural form. The framework, as well as the beams and original pine plank walls, now form the backdrop for a luminous and airy lifestyle, filled with

The importance of the passageway in this unique home on the Îles de la Madeleine is clear as soon as you enter the house. The complex angles and the horizontal and vertical lines of the cedar and the Douglas fir create texture and movement. Furka, a silkscreen by Robert Wolfe, a great friend of the couple, hangs above the fireplace. Its circular motion seems to capture the serenity and vivacity of the house (left). Everything is perfect in the passageway: the form, the materials, the architectural details, and the charm of the islands (right).

a natural freshness. The decoration is also simple; here the "basics" are the preferred style, with clear surfaces, a few chairs, a table, contemporary furniture, and a sofa. The bare walls are adorned with abstract art pieces and hundreds of books. The living area on the ground floor fulfills the double role of living room and kitchen. It is decorated simply, with highlights of yellow and pale green. Even the lighting is discreet in this immaculate world. The kitchen island is the only imposing element; it is a veritable distillation of modern efficiency. It was designed by YH2, as was the built-in furniture and office tables on the mezzanine.

The magic comes from the entryways, which perpetuate the game of hide-and-seek. This is a place where several people can live without necessarily running into each other. Whimsy is also present behind the kitchen island, where a small secret staircase leads from the ground floor to the basement. This has been turned into an apartment where guests can come and go as they please. This well-lit apartment includes bedrooms, a bathroom, a dining room, and a living room.

A made to measure oasis

The new building was placed at a twenty-degree angle to the main structure; with the passageway, it creates an intimate windbreak. It houses the master bedroom and bath, and also has a private entrance. Here, the style is more "Japanese serenity," an effect emphasized by the sparse furnishings. The residents prefer the immensity of nature, which they can contemplate from the large tub in the bathroom. The upper bedroom contains only a bed, a mattress, and many books.

The covered passageway is an unusual element in the traditional architecture of these islands. But it is essential in that it functions as a link, a break, and an observation station. The unique arrangement of the floorboards in a small section of the main living area floor forms a line that repeats the axis of the passageway, which is situated behind another door at the end of the room. Once through this door, we cross the passage leading to an oasis of tranquility. "It's amazing, we close the doors, and no one hears anything from either side of the passageway," says the owner.

The residents believe that it is possible to be original and create a residence that does not distort the environment. The sudden interest that people are now showing in their home is proof of this, and since it has been renovated, people are constantly walking by, cameras in hand. All that was missing for this house to vibrate in synch with the island's tune was a clothesline. A lack that has since been remedied.

RENDEZVOUS

NATHALIE ROY

QUÉBÉCOIS HOSPITALITY

A manor house and a rebuilt mill at the Auberge Le Baluchon in La Mauricie (preceding pages). The traditional breakfast during the sugaring season includes, among other dishes, tourtière*, sausages, and omelet (above). The tent of the Aventure Mikuan II camp in the heart of Saguenay offers a welcome refuge (facing page).

Visitors love the proverbial Québécois hospitality. Open-minded and interested in everything, most Quebeckers are charming and like to talk and share experiences. Indeed, the Québécois host is delighted to have visitors and makes sure that they remember him in highly flattering terms. You'll therefore feel perfectly at home, whether you're staying in small or large hotels, in the countryside or the city, in a cozy or modest inn, a bed-and-breakfast in the country or on the coast, or motels or guesthouses (when you may stay in a family's spare room).

Quebec is the place to come for freedom and an oversized environment. This immense territory offers a natural setting that encompasses the dense untamed forest of La Mauricie and Saguenay; the Laurentian forest, which is flamboyant in the autumn, a veritable Impressionist canvas of warm tones; and the lush green hills, fields, and vineyards of the Eastern Townships. Visitors also come to explore the sandbars and mountains of the Gaspé Peninsula and the rugged beauty of the Îles de la Madeleine clouded over with the mist known locally as *salange**. There is also a marvelous quality in the lifestyle of villages lining the banks of the St. Lawrence River, as well as a tremendous energy in the large cities that encompass so much history and modernism. Quebec City, the provincial capital, is one such city, as is the multicultural Montreal, with its urban landscape unlike any other place in the world.

Within these diverse landscapes, the quality of accommodations can range from frugal to astonishingly luxurious, but they are always charming. Along with the usual uniform and characterless chains, the selection is vast, and visitors have such a wide range of choices that regardless of the planned itinerary or budget, they will always find what they're looking for. Outside the cities, hospitality generally means rural comfort and is based on outdoor activities, rest, and culture. Once you move nearer to the coast, this same hospitality becomes disarmingly simple and lends itself to perfect relaxation; this is a brand of hospitality to savor in small doses of peaceful happiness—gazing at the lovely St. Lawrence River or, farther to the east, the sea.

Historical residences are common, with the Château Frontenac topping the list. Here, the staff awaits guests to the sumptuous hotel in full livery. This type of luxury establishment offers a dream stay, situated in a historical structure. Others exist in smaller cities and even calm little villages. In addition, in larger cities you can find avant-garde and dynamic places to stay in the form of boutique hotels, where the concept of comfort goes so far as to include made-to-order mattresses and the possibility of actually purchasing a piece of furniture or decorative object that

The forest, and antique gardens at the Domain Joly-De Lotbinière and the 1851 manor house along the St. Lawrence River at Pointe Platon in the St. Lawrence Plain are all in keeping with the picturesque movement of the nineteenth century (left). The Seigneurie des Aulnaies at Saint-Roch-des-Aulnaies in Lower St. Lawrence is a neoclassical seigneurial manor that also reflects the Victorian era (right).

catches a guest's eye. And finally, Québécois hospitality can also be a rustic, rural environment, out in the wide-open territory dotted with one million lakes.

Travelers taking their first trip to Quebec will be surprised to discover a country that strives to maintain its European roots within a decidedly North American context. This duality is unique in this region, and Quebec is a fertile land for a number of innovations ranging from the technological to the artistic, notably in multimedia and the decorative arts. Blown glass and pottery, for example, have achieved international renown. Craftsmanship is the best ambassador of Québécois expertise, while it also promotes traditional production techniques. Even today, visitors can admire locally made objects such as the *catalogne**, the arrowhead sash* and the quilt, to mention just a few examples.

Remembering the past is essential in Quebec, particularly in the architectural domain, with such examples as the Manoir Mauvide-Genest and the Manoir Papineau, two restored manor houses which both reflect the comfortable lifestyles that were characteristic of their respective periods. Memory also plays a role in the preservation of other traditions, such as the ancestral customs of a Huron village, Onhoüa Chetek8E, a society based on the native wisdom that existed long before the arrival of the Europeans.

Quebeckers are also bons vivants who appreciate life's pleasures. They devote time and energy to creating areas where the beauty of large natural spaces can be appreciated and preserved. And after any outdoor adventure, a stop for a good meal is also a must, whether it's a leisurely lunch in the country or a great restaurant. Québécois wine, cheese, beer, and cider will top off a memorable day. Visitors should take time to taste everything, as the regional cuisine is also a major part of the Québécois experience. A wide range of tastes, flavors and textures exist, from the hearty *poutine** (French fries covered with melted cheese and gravy) to the delicate sea urchin cream. All in all, the diverse fare contributes to the charm of a visit.

It's time to continue our trip to the heart of Québécois hospitality. Your new home is delighted to have you.

TRADITION AND MODERNITY: LUXURY ACCOMMODATION

The most prestigious and luxurious establishments are rich in history, and have been precursors of the flourishing tourist industry in Quebec. Created from the vision of the powerful and elitist owners, these resorts have, fortunately, become far more democratic. They offer cozy comfort with all the amenities of modern life, but with the added benefit of discretion. These elegant hotels and inns are beautifully decorated and often feature acclaimed restaurants. Here, dreams become memorable realities.

PRESTIGIOUS ESTABLISHMENTS

The railway was the cornerstone of Canada's economic development. It also contributed to the growth of a new type of tourism, in an era when travel was generally reserved for an elite who wanted to discover the magnificent landscapes. "If we can't export the landscape, we'll import the traveler," said William Van Horne, president of the Canadian Pacific Railway at the time. This company constructed the Château Frontenac. The three hotels built along the St. Lawrence River—the Château Frontenac, the Manoir Richelieu, and the Hôtel Tadoussac— are all proud symbols of this era.

Elegant comfort in the Charlevoix region: the Manoir Richelieu

The Manoir Richelieu was at the height of its glory during the age of the luxury steamboats, nicknamed the "white boats," which sailed down the St. Lawrence River toward Tadoussac. In 1899, this sumptuous establishment on the cliffs of Pointe-au-Pic, at La Malbair in the Charlevoix region, was a favorite haunt of members of both American and Canadian high society. The Manoir Richelieu was originally built with cedar shingles, Nathalie Grondin tells us, but was destroyed by fire. It was immediately reconstructed in concrete. The design was inspired by those of châteaux in Normandy; it features large, fairly austere surfaces, which are offset by immense windows and setbacks on the façade. No detail, regardless of how small or luxurious, was overlooked during the major restoration of the vast succession of lobbies and arcades in 1998. The deep, rich colors of the materials used, the gleaming light fixtures, and the dark wood and reddish-brown paneling in the Murray Room, for example, all contribute to the exclusive and elegant comfort that authentically reproduces the hotel's golden age in the 1930s.

The fireplace in the Le Champlain dining room at the Château Frontenac in Quebec City features a magnificent interior of reddish-brown woodwork and carved paneling adorned with heraldic signs.

It's teatime at the
Manoir Richelieu at
La Malbaie near
Quebec City. And
rather than stroll
over to the casino
of this prestigious
establishment,
relaxed visitors
may prefer the
indoor terrace,
where they can
enjoy unforgettable
moments sampling
the delicious dishes
and enjoying the
splendid view over
the St. Lawrence
River.

The brass elevators at the Château Frontenac in Quebec City lead to the twenty-four floors of the tower designed by Montreal architect Maxwell in 1924.

The Château Frontenac, overlooking Quebec City

This distinctive hotel has 618 rooms. It has hosted movie stars, monarchs, heads of state, and other famous figures. Since it opened in 1893, it has participated in memorable events for numerous people in Quebec, along with some of history's most tragic moments, including preparations for the D-Day landings. The hotel fulfilled its role as a country house for a wealthy clientele, although the establishment became a public favorite and eventually, an El Dorado for the middle class.

Designed by the New York architect Bruce Price, the French-style hotel was built in 1893 atop Cap Diamant in Quebec City. At the time, it had only two wings: the Riverview and the Saint Louis wings. Its success required the addition

of the Citadelle and Pavillon Citadelle wings, designed by the same architect in 1899. Finally, in 1924, the Château Frontenac acquired the appearance that is known throughout the world today, with the construction of the famous central tower by the Maxwell brothers, renowned Montreal architects. As the symbol of a people, the Château Frontenac combines tradition and modernity, splendor and sobriety. Gleaming brass, oak, and marble create an ambiance of lasting elegance. The warmth radiating from the alabaster lights softens the austerity of the cornices, the Scottish-style coffered paneling, and the Jacobin-style furniture. An avid historian, Christine Marcoux guides us through the alterations in the hotel, notably the transformation of rooms from one function to another. We now understand why the current restaurant, Le Champlain, features such lavish woodwork, as it was once the main entrance, before the central tower was built.

The Van Horne suite (the former private apartment of the owner, William Van Horne) is in the Citadelle wing. It still has the original furnishings, including two magnificent fireplaces and Delft porcelain. The liveried staff provides the same discreet and irreproachable service as in times past, the hallmark of this great international hotel.

The Hôtel Tadoussac on the Saguenay Fjord

Near the Saguenay Fjord in Côte Nord, a large red-roofed hotel stretches out along one of the most beautiful bays in the world, the Bay of Tadoussac (or Totouskak, in the language of the First Nations, which means breasts, an allusion to the two round hills to the west of the village). The first hotel was constructed in 1867 and destroyed in 1941. In 1942, William Hugh Coverdale, the president of the Canada Steamship Lines and owner of the Manoir Richelieu, had the Hôtel Tadoussac rebuilt. The white wooden rectangular building was constructed in the vernacular style, hence its blend of styles, Second Empire with a mansard roof.

"The hotel is a synthesis of comfort and nature that must be conserved," says Tina Tremblay, who has been at the hotel for more than fifteen years. Even today, life at the hotel revolves around hikes in the forest, whale watching, and skiing on the nearby dunes, among other outdoor activities. But lounging on the terrace, gazing out over the bay, and reading a good book are still favorite pastimes.

The elegant lobby is decorated in a simple blue and gold décor. It's a perfect setting for relaxing and discovering history, through the old photographs and the period objects. In addition, the original details in the dining room, including the paneling, frescoes, and hand-painted motifs, add a touch of warmth and refinement. The comfortable rooms are decorated around a nautical theme, and the river is omnipresent in life at Tadoussac. The romantic charm of the hotel and the beauty of untamed nature are irresistible.

A period scene in tones of blue and green in the Coverdale dining room at the Hôtel Tadoussac in Côte Nord (above, top). View of the bay and the chapel, which was built in 1747 (above, bottom).

BOUTIQUE HOTELS

Boutique hotels have become a flourishing trend over the last decade. They target a demanding and sophisticated clientele. Situated in urban settings and often housed in charming older buildings, these hotels are highly prized among discerning travelers, especially professionals. These hotels combine the great service of large hotels with the personalized service of smaller ones. They often have no more than fifty or so rooms and tend to be characterized by a contemporary, modern luxury and décor that set them apart from other establishments. Designed to offer a high level of comfort, boutique hotels are also equipped with the latest technology to meet the demands of their working guests.

The name "boutique" comes from the fact that they are small with highly personalized service. They constitute a rapidly growing trend, and in Quebec this type of hotel features magnificent architectural designs and interiors. Indeed, many of them are well known far beyond the borders of Quebec. The following two hotels provide a glimpse into a very contemporary, sophisticated side of Montreal.

The visual serenity of a hotel in Old Montreal

Inaugurated in 2002, the Hôtel Gault has done everything it can to eliminate its "picturesque" side. The historical reference of this building, constructed in Old Montreal in 1871, starts and ends at the lovely Second Empire façade. Once you step through the door, the memory of Andrew Gault's import-export company evaporates in the contemporary prism of the YH2 architects.

Mariette Parent is one of the founders of the Gault, along with Ghyslain Langlois, one of the hotel's managers. "Our professional clientele appreciates the beauty of the materials and the spaces," says Parent, especially as some of them are designers and architects themselves. She believes, however, that architecture is secondary to the comfort of her guests. Comfort at the Gault also involves visual serenity. "Hotels are often over-decorated, and I don't like that. It was therefore natural to design minimalist spaces," explains Loukas Yiacouvakis of YH2. Despite the multipurpose nature of the ground floor, it nevertheless remains very intimate; it has a reception area, a place to relax, and, behind the fireplace, a reading room. This latter area is elevated, and the warmer materials—wood and fabric—create a psychological barrier.

The thirty-room hotel is appealing not only for its esthetics, but also for the simple everyday enjoyment of opening the windows in the room to get a feel for the neighborhood, contemplating the begonias on the windows, and ordering whatever you like for breakfast. Each room feels like a private loft space; some have been designed for short stays, while others are more suitable for long-term occupation. They were created as spaces for relaxation as well as work. Hence, the architects

The clean lines and modern design of the lobby of the Hôtel Gault in Old Montreal (facing page) are replicated in this loft and room under the eaves (above).

The shutters are closed in the small living room of a suite in the Hôtel Saint-Paul in Old Montreal. The semidarkness adds to the intimacy of the boudoir and the harmony of shapes and colors (above).

Luminosity and languor come together in discreet luxury in this bedroom in the Hôtel Saint-Paul. The diaphanous, fluid material creates an extremely feminine style (facing page).

designed changeable spaces, in which wood, curtains, and sliding furniture create intimate and clearly defined areas. Decorating requires considerable thought, and for Parent, who earned a master's degree in fine arts, objects are her passion. She selects them not only for their esthetics, but also for their functionality and durability. The Gault is in constant flux and is not just a showcase for the great classics of twentieth-century design—notably copies of work by Pierre Paulin and Charles Eames—but is also a forum for young Québécois designers, thanks to the creation of a collection containing their artwork.

Shadow, light, and raw materials at the Hôtel Saint-Paul

The Hôtel Saint Paul is concealed behind the Beaux-Arts façade of this large building, constructed in 1908 to house the headquarters of Canadian Express, the financial institution of the Canadian railways. Situated in Old Montreal and opened in 1998, the 120-room hotel was created by interior designer Ana Borallo of Ancanto Interiors.

The ground floor had been occupied by offices, and a suspended ceiling concealed some of the windows. "It's fortunate that there was no carved woodwork, as it would have been sad to have had to remove it," says Arnaud Marande, who keeps an eye on the image of the Saint-Paul. The various views over the city inspired the designer: "The neutral interior underscores the architecture outside, such as the stone cornices that you can see from the windows." Borallo wanted to unify these two dimensions and conceived of a highly personal stylistic representation of the five elements. The raw materials used, such as marble and limestone, reinforce this idea of extending the outside to the inside. Guests penetrate into a world of light and darkness; the fields of shadow and light, the steel, and the monochromatic shades evoke the fluidity of metal and water. The bedrooms offer another sensory experience. The soft natural fabrics, the palette of neutral colors, and the contemporary and primitive furniture—pieces by designer Érik Desprez made from hundred-year-old beams—all express the comfort of the nourishing earth and the warmth of wood. Sobriety is the watchword at the Saint-Paul, although the designer's love of fashion comes through in her selection of fabrics, notably wool, raw silk, silk taffeta, and silk velvet, all fabrics used in the clothing industry. She has also highlighted some of the space, like the bedrooms, with lovely draped curtains.

Visitors are fascinated by this hotel and often come to pick up some new ideas, measuring-tape or camera in hand. The Cube restaurant and Cru du Saint-Paul bar are also popular spots to see and be seen but also to blend incognito into the background, behind the alabaster fireplace in the lobby, where a small alcove has been designed. The ambience is cozy, and the silence is barely broken by the murmuring of soft voices. This small sitting room blends both warm and cold elements with a sense of voluptuousness. The rich, intense colors of the decorative accessories are perfectly adapted to the symbolic purity of fire and ice in the fireplace.

Intimacy at the Hôtel Saint-Paul in Old Montreal is created by contrasts: the soft sensuality of the bedrooms is complemented by the more vivacious tones of the fire in the Cru bar.

INNS, GUESTHOUSES, AND POURVOIRIES

Inns, guesthouses, B & Bs, motels, and *pourvoiries** are legion in Quebec. These types of establishment, like the four hundred outfitters, members of the Fédération des Pourvoiries du Québéc, give visitors an exceptional opportunity to commune with nature. They offer accommodation and all the services related to outdoor activities, hunting, and fishing. The more rustic places are surprisingly friendly, while other more luxury establishments offer a higher level of service as well as incomparable gourmet food. Two boutique guesthouses, mirrors of contemporary Quebec, have garnered much attention, offering serious competition to their urban counterparts: Bleu-sur-Mer and Au Salange.

Comfort and tranquility at Bleu-sur-Mer in the Gaspé Peninsula

Bleu-sur-Mer, an inn for discerning travelers, is located at Port Daniel in the Baie des Chaleurs on the Gaspé Peninsula. Opened in 2002 by the lawyer Benoît Pilon and graphic designer Micheline Roy from Montreal, the inn features three large sound-proofed rooms with soft beds. It offers an exceptional level of comfort, modulated by the surrounding presence of water, with the sea in front and the sandbar behind. The dream rooms in this respectable Edwardian residence, built in 1902, combine lux-ury, nature, and sophistication. The owner's mission is clear: to adapt contemporary design to a heritage structure. The original architectural elements, such as the mon-umental cherry-wood staircase, share the interior with glass floats, Indonesian furniture, and contemporary artwork by Gaspé painters. "It was important to make it an inti-mate, personal place," says Benoît Pilon. Every evening, the hosts and guests share a pre-dinner drink. The owners have also instituted a "lazy parent" service: they take care of their customers' children, while the parents get a chance to relax.

Au Salange: an unusual setting on the Îles de la Madeleine

The sea is omnipresent at Au Salange, forming a backdrop to the vast luminous spaces. The bed-and-breakfast is situated in Havre aux Maisons on the Îles de la Madeleine, in a remote location known as Pointe Basse. The owners, Dominique Gagnon and his partner Édith Grégoire, are both avid travelers. In 1999, they designed the décor, which has echoes of the exoticism of Madras and Bali, com-bined with the maritime charm of the Îles de la Madeleine. "We wanted to offer something different from the Victorian style," says Dominique Gagnon. The carved driftwood furniture, decorative objects from the regional Artisans du Sable, and sea charts have been combined with contemporary glass and metal. The three com-fortable rooms feature unusual elements, such as technical equipment posing as bedside tables or fence posts serving as holders for the thick bath towels.

Bleu-sur-Mer, an inn constructed in 1902 at Port Daniel on the Gaspé Peninsula, is a combination of classical luxury and contemporary design (above). The Grande Bleue at the Salange Inn offers a view over the immense Îles de la Madeleine landscape.

Ice fishing in La Mauricie at the Hotel Sacacomie

Guests arrive at this trendy refuge, located at Saint-Alexis-des-Monts in La Mauricie, by seaplane or car. The three-mile (five-kilometer) mountain road carved from the rocky hillside winds through spectacular landscapes. Lake Sacacomie appears out of nowhere some two miles (three kilometers) from the hotel. By the time we reach the hotel, we feel as if we're at the end of the world. The 105-room hotel opened in 1996. It was constructed on a rocky outcrop that overlooks a vast forest and Lake Sacacomie, which has a coastline of twenty-four miles (forty kilometers). The hotel complex lies next to the Réserve Faunique Mastigouche and encompasses several lakes and hiking trails. There are plenty of outdoor activities all year round.

During the winter, nature seems to be indomitable, and we admire the infinite landscape. The ice-fishing expedition was a total success, and on request, the hotel will be serving the trout we caught on the frozen lake for our dinner. We return happily to the imposing log house, with its steep roof and gable windows, balconies, and large terraces. "We can fulfill any whim and work to maintain a peaceful atmosphere," says manager Colombe Bourque. The tranquil setting is a perfect place to rest and recuperate, free from television, radio, and paparazzi, which is much appreciated by visitors, professionals, artists, and politicians. The staff takes care of everything with discretion. During summer evenings, the balconies remain in semi-darkness to protect privacy.

The owner, Yvon Plante, from Saint-Alexis-des-Monts, designed the sober wood architecture featuring pine, rugged natural elements, and soft and sensual materials like fur. His aim was to blend into the environment. This impression stays with us as we reach the Père suite, furnished in a highly contemporary style. It includes a sitting room, a dining room, bedrooms, and bathrooms. Looking out of large windows and past the immense terrace, we see that nature is clearly the main dish here, served up with elegance and simplicity.

The chalets of the Pourvoirie Cap au Leste

The Saguenay Fjord is a must-see for travelers seeking the ultimate remote location. Perched at six hundred and sixty feet (two hundred meters), the Pourvoirie Cap au Leste offers a magnificent view over the pine and maple forest as well as the fjord. The isolated site is some nine miles (fifteen kilometers) from the village of Sainte-Rose-du-Nord. Cap au Leste is a recreation of an old logging camp.

"We stressed the settler aspect, in honor of our pioneers," says the director, Louise Nadeau. It's a concept well suited to the location, which was still nothing more than a forest in 1998. The site was only cleared in certain places to make room for the future buildings, to link the *pourvoirie* to the four-mile (seven-kilometer) road, and to create hiking trails. The ambiance is authentic, with chalets built of

The bedrooms (above, top) at the Hôtel Sacacomie in La Mauricie (facing page) are cozy and comfortable. A pioneering spirit sets the tone at the Montagnais cabin at Cap au Leste in the Saguenay region (above, bottom).

Le Baluchon, an inn in La Mauricie, is a Victorian structure (above). View of the fjord from the immense Algonquin chalet at Cap au Leste in the Saguenay region (facing page).

traditional squared timber, rustic furniture, and old utilitarian objects. The main chalet has a large dining room and open kitchen, modeled after the *cookerie** of a logging camp. During winter months, visitors like to gather here after a long day outside to savor a delicious hot soup. The five guest chalets each have a shared living room, a slow-combustion stove, from three to ten bedrooms, and individual bathrooms.

It is a congenial place. "We create a friendly environment. We treat our guests as if they were members of the family," says Louise Nadeau. A guest sitting comfortably nearby, feet on the low table, confirms her point.

After a snowmobile excursion on the frozen lake, there's nothing more luxurious than returning to a chalet to bask in the heat of a roaring fire. It's a special extra touch provided by the staff, which takes the edge off the severe winter conditions. A long hike on snowshoes creates a special rhythm to the afternoon, while in the distance we hear the musher* cajoling his sled dogs.

A rustic ambiance in La Mauricie at the Auberge Le Baluchon

In 1982, a group of seven students opened Le Baluchon, based on an ecological-outdoors concept that was totally unknown in Quebec. After many disappointments and problems, due to a lack of investors—the group of students soon dropped to just two, who were called dreamers—the establishment gradually grew to become a highly prized destination for its overall approach to "gastronomy, the outdoors, and culture." Situated at Saint-Paulin, at the entrance of La Mauricie, and built on the land of the Magnan Falls Hydroelectric Interpretation Centre and Park, Le Baluchon offers a unique environmental experience and a totally relaxing vacation.

"The site is divided into four sectors; each one represents a season and is based on the five senses," explains Yves Savard, the founder, along with his partner Louis Lessard. The ninety-room establishment includes three inns and a chalet. There are waterfalls, islands and archipelago, plains, groves, and wooded hillsides stretching over nearly sixteen miles (twenty-eight kilometers) of marked trails along the river. The architecture of the buildings has something of the Victorian style, along with elements from old farmhouses. Gabled windows, wrought iron, and shutters contribute to the friendly ambiance. "Everything must be coherent and esthetic," says Savard. As proof, the interiors are a skillful mix of modernism, rural styles, and bourgeois interiors, with fabric decorating the walls. The inn also has a manor house and a mill, constructed as a set for a television series. Various companies joined forces with the pair, notably a microbrewery, which makes beer from wheat and buckwheat.

After enjoying a copious meal at the Baluchon restaurant, we set out on an expedition on skates, following a trail for three miles (five kilometers) on the Rivière du Loup.

The charm of "crazy quilts" in the bedrooms of the Vieux Foyer bed-and-breakfast on Île d'Orléans near Quebec City (right). This rare oval table in the dining room dates from 1750 (below).

A bed-and-breakfast in a former farm on the Île d'Orléans

The blue eyes of former computer specialist Daniel Boucher shine as he speaks of his bed-and-breakfast, Au Vieux Foyer. He discovered it in 1989 and, as he was a frequent guest, learned that it was to be sold. In 1990, he purchased the establishment, which was filled with antiques collected over the years by the former owner and his children. It had also served as a museum for thirty years. The bed-and-breakfast makes him as happy as his guests, who are delighted to enjoy such a new experience.

The old wood-plank house with gabled windows seems to be frozen in time, an architectural souvenir from the end of French rule. It's worth a trip just to see the building. For the traveler looking for history on the bucolic Île d'Orléans, the attraction of the old walls with peeling paint and worn staircases is irresistible. "I want to keep the Vieux Foyer as it is, for the value of its heritage," says Boucher. "We all need something stable in our lives." His decision sometimes creates a few problems, as it's hard to reconcile the rugged farmhouse style with modern comforts and design. In 1996, he remodeled the bathrooms to make them more comfortable. The rooms, including four bedrooms, are all decorated in the nineteenth-century style, with antique (and often rare) furniture, *catalognes* (woven throw rugs), and old-fashioned colors. The epicenter of the Vieux Foyer is the summer kitchen. This is the domain of the eccentric owner. Before taking off for a walk toward the distant river, the guests gather in the morning around a U-shaped table, where the owner launches into an obligatory philosophical conversation. "I make busy people slow down. We all eat together here, as a big family," says Boucher. "Comfort comes from a good long sleep and a hearty breakfast."

The magic of this bed-and-breakfast also comes from the legends and creaking old floors. One day, a young boy walking with his mother whispered, "We can't stay here, Mom. There are ghosts."

River view at the Auberge du Mange Grenouille

A magnificent red house decorated with painted white friezes awaits in the heart of Le Bic village in Lower St. Lawrence. In 1990, Carole Faucher and Jean Rossignol purchased this rundown building, a former warehouse constructed in 1843. The owners, two former actors with a wide experience in the theater, transformed the place into an acclaimed inn.

The twenty-two-room inn offers several striking views of the river and Bic Islands. The garden and pavilion behind the inn is a favorite spot among guests. The disarray forms a charming site: irises, daisies, rudbeckias, and wild roses have been allowed to twine around the fountains and sculptures. This natural profusion extends into the operetta interiors.

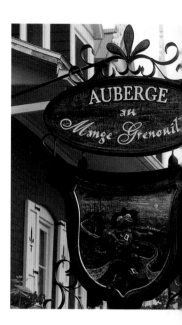

People come from far and wide to visit the picturesque village of Bic in Lower St. Lawrence and to enjoy the romantic experience and unforgettable food at the acclaimed Auberge du Mange Grenouille (top). The lush garden behind the inn is a beautiful place to relax among the flowers and fountains (bottom). The elegant and discreetly sensual Victorian style of the attic: in room number seven, the central decorative element is this imposing bed, possibly in the American Renaissance Revival style, circa 1870–1900 (following page).

Fragments of brocade, lace, and velvet create an aura of romanticism and Victorian theatricality in the older part of the inn. The cozy atmosphere in one of the sitting rooms is a perfect place for intimate conversations. They often grow into loud whispers as the guests move to the candlelit dining room. The owners devoted a great deal of time to creating these effects. The same goes for the bedrooms. The small attic room decorated with faded green has old books and photographs. Another room features the dusty pink tones of a romantic boudoir with period decorative objects. "Our lifestyle is expressed in the decoration," says Carole Faucher. The artwork and books all contribute to the effect. The bedrooms in the newer part of the inn facing the garden are designed with a fresh touch, favoring fluidity, textures, and natural materials such as linen and cotton.

It's wonderful to stay at the Mange Grenouille as it is a sum of multiple sensory pleasures that grow from one room to the next, not to mention the pleasures of the table. The owners are extremely attentive to their guests, as Faucher says, smiling, "Innkeeper, time for a drink!"—her sixth sense reading our minds.

The Gîte du Mont-Albert, in the natural setting of the Gaspé Peninsula

The road from the southern section of the Parc National de la Gaspésie climbs nearly sixty miles (one hundred kilometers), through a remote stretch of conifers, before reaching the Gîte du Mont-Albert at the base of Mont Albert. Via the northern road, it is a few miles from Sainte-Anne-des-Monts, a small village.

Run by the national park, the hotel first opened in 1937, offering accommodation for visitors seeking remote natural spaces. The Gîte du Mont-Albert is a gigantic window open to nature, "the soul of the establishment," says the director David Dubreuil. The white painted building is characteristic of governmental structures from the period, with a steep roofline, gabled windows, and pinnacle turrets, an architectural mirror of the surrounding sea of mountains. The 2002 renovation was undertaken with a respect for the spirit of the place: "public spaces oriented around the landscape," in Dubreuil's words.

The establishment also has nineteen chalets in addition to the hotel rooms. The first, dating to the 1950s, were used to house the park rangers. All are attractive, especially chalet number one with a pretty bedroom under the eaves.

The warmth of wood and leather greets us at the check-in desk. We stand silent as we look around the large, serene interior area, an elegantly simple and rugged place. We drop off our luggage and head for the bar. The high ceilings here seem to be heading off to join the mountains. The architecture repeats elements from the dining room, including the beams, stone fireplace, and visible iron fittings. The bar is everyone's favorite spot, as it is the perfect place to sit and watch the sunset, relaxing in one of the comfortable armchairs.

The bar of the Gîte du Mont-Albert is a favorite place to sit and contemplate the rugged alpine landscape of the Parc National de la Gaspésie (above, top). The inn offers total relaxation (above, bottom).

The perfect way to end a stroll through the gardens of the Manoir Hovey in North Hatley, in the Eastern Townships, is at the exquisite restaurant (above, left). Farther away, a small romantic chalet houses the luxurious and isolated Cartier suite (above, right). It includes a lovely deck and private beach on Lac Massawippi (right).

The amazing colonial architecture of the Manoir Hovey

We have reached an establishment not far from North Hatley in the Eastern Townships. It combines three influences: English and American architectural styles and French culinary expertise. The private driveway winds through a lovely forest and past a few picturesque ponds. Suddenly, the Manoir Hovey appears. The colonial architecture, constructed at the base of a mountain facing Lake Masssawippi, looks surprising in this northern climate.

The overall ambiance is "floral and romantic," according to owner Stephen Stafford. Constructed in 1900 as a summer home by Henry Atkinson, a rich industrialist who fled the United States, "The Birches" is reminiscent of George Washington's residence in Mount Vernon, Virginia. In 1959, the property opened as the Manoir Hovey. In 1979, Kathryn and Stephen Stafford purchased the establishment, which now has forty rooms, and proceeded to transform it into a luxurious refuge.

The main building, a former coach house, and the other outbuildings (which became suites) form an elegant and harmonious complex. "We wanted to preserve the history and charm of the place; it's impossible to detect the additions we've made," says Stafford. The vaulted ceilings, the canopy beds, and the rich curtains draped over the windows all contribute to the luxury and elegance of the place. The contrasts are clear in the more rustic Tap Room, the former stables transformed into a pub. It has a fireplace made of 10,000 bricks and many objects, including a magnificent birch-bark canoe. This object gives us the idea that if the ghost of Plumley le Baron, one of the pioneers of the village of North Hatley, ever decided to announce his return by ringing the reception bell, we would go down to the beach for a canoe trip on the lake—where we could stop in a isolated bay and enjoy the sumptuous picnic basket prepared by our charming hosts.

Auberge Hatley, a prestigious establishment overlooking the lake

The pretty town of North Hatley, situated in the Eastern Townships, has hundreds of treasures, including the Auberge Hatley, which overlooks Lake Massawippi. This former summer residence was constructed in the early twentieth century. It became an inn in the 1960s, and since 2002 has been a member of the Groupe Germain. This family-run Quebec company, created in 1987, owns several hotels, including the Dominion 1912 in Quebec City. The Auberge Hatley is distinctive for a variety of refined touches, ranging from the quality of the service to its famed restaurant, which was a decisive factor in the success of this member of the Relais et Châteaux group, as Christiane Germain, one of the owners, tells us. The elegant entrance to the hotel illustrates everything guests seek here: a luxurious lifestyle and beautiful

Guests at the Auberge Hatley in North Hatley in the Eastern Townships (top) enjoy the good life on Lac Massawippi and its cozy sitting room before dining in the highly acclaimed restaurant (bottom).

Pierre Faucher has recreated an old-time village at the Sucrerie de la Montagne in Rigaud, in the St. Lawrence Plain, to promote the typical atmosphere of the "good ol' times" in Quebec.

landscapes. The many windows and back porch are stepping-stones to the natural calm outside, pleasant hikes, and more private moments in the garden or on the lake.

The classical interior design combines floral motifs and stripes, creating a pastoral look. The decoration consists of a few paintings, some engravings, and souvenirs from the village. "The ambiance here is chameleon-like; during the summer the rooms are filled with sunlight, while the winter months are cozier and more intimate," says Germain. The entire hotel, from the bar to the dining room and the lobby, is devoted to the discreet satisfaction of its guests' needs. The twenty-five comfortable rooms are decorated according to diverse themes, including one with Provencal motifs and another English-style room in shades of green. It is such a haven of peace and tranquility that a number of faithful guests have literally appropriated certain rooms. Even before leaving, they reserve "their" room for a future trip.

A Québécois village from the past: the Sucrerie de la Montagne

Pierre Faucher, a big strong man with a flourishing white beard, is the perfect image of a Québécois lumberman. "I stopped shaving during the construction of the Sucrerie, it was all just coincidence," he says. In his twenties, he left his region—the Beauce a part of Quebec famous for its resourceful and determined inhabitants—to travel and work around the world. Once he returned to Quebec, he decided he wanted to return to a traditional way of life. "I guess that learning about other cultures made me realize the importance of my own heritage," says Faucher.

While he was working as a consultant for a large company, Pierre Faucher decided to find a way to bring together his work and nature and to promote his country. In 1979, he built his own sugarhouse* cabin from barn wood, which he furnished with an old stove, a few tables, some picturesque tools and objects, and family portraits. The place was such a success that Faucher decided to transform it into a replica of an early Québécois village.

Situated in Rigaud in the St. Lawrence Plain, the Sucrerie de la Montagne now includes the sugarhouse cabin and two dining rooms, a bakery, and a general store. One of the most charming aspects of the place is that the maple trees are tapped as in the early days, and that the sap is still collected by hand, bucket by bucket. Faucher also has three rustic log cabins, which he constructed in the middle of the maple tree grove. The only way to reach his place is by wagon in the summer and sleigh in the winter. These romantic cabins are furnished simply: the warmth of the woven curtains, *catalognes*, rustic furniture, and antique objects all revive the dream of returning to country life. The rugged and soft materials form harmonious blends as you sit in front of a blazing fireplace. It's a completely new experience for foreign visitors, who discover with amazement this utterly authentic environment—because Pierre Faucher, an ambassador of tradition, does everything for real.

Settlers in Nouvelle France wanted to build a new world. The simplicity of this rustic cabin at the Sucrerie de la Montagne offers a comfortable haven. Rest for the body and soul comes in a modest guise on this mezzanine.

COMFORT IN THE EXTREME COLD

In Quebec, people say there are only two seasons: winter and July. Complaining about winter is part of local tradition, but residents get a certain measure of satisfaction in this, as if having conquered a particularly arduous winter proves how tough they are. Winter is a magical season, whether you spend it indoors, your feet stretched out in front of a roaring fire, or bundled up and outside practicing the art of survival in arctic conditions.

The ephemeral and magical Ice Hotel

"Sleeping in an igloo is the ultimate contact with winter," says Jacques Desbois, founder of the Ice Hotel located at Sainte-Catherine-de-la-Jacques-Cartier, just a few minutes from Quebec City. "I began with the construction of *queenzhy** and started getting my children to sleep in an igloo." He opened the Ice Hotel in 2002. People come for all kinds of reasons: conferences, events, entertainment, diversion, or to experience a "reassuring and gentle adventure," as he puts it.

The fairy tale begins within the hotel walls, a complex of wide corridors and inner courtyards covering a surface area of 32,300 square feet (3,000 square meters). We walk over the powder snow on the floor, trying to sort through a host of contradictory impressions. During the day, the sunlight should provide some heat, but the primary sensation is that of cold and immobility. At night, however, we are wrapped in intimacy, thanks to the system of fiber optic lighting. The most beautiful time to stay at the hotel is in February to see the sunrises and sunsets: the sun's rays reflect off the snow and carved ice into a prism of blues, mauves, and greens. Just about everything about this architecture is ephemeral. The structure is extremely complex to build, despite the basic shapes and massive volumes.

Sculptors furnish the hotel with a myriad of decorative and useful objects. The ambiance in the wedding chapel is surreal, with champagne served in glasses cut from the ice, not to mention the bar with alcoves cut directly into the walls. It's also hard to believe that a real fire burns in the fireplace, without producing any heat.

The suites and bedrooms are actually luxury bivouacs. The beds are made of ice, with an ingenious lighting system under the bed. A wood panel has then been placed atop the ice, along with a mattress covered with fur and then a sleeping bag. It makes for a perfectly restful and deep night's sleep. In the morning, we hear, it's positively euphoric to wake up to a steaming cup of hot chocolate or coffee.

Trapper cabins and tents in Saguenay

What do you find in a prospector's tent in −40° F (−40° C) weather? As tourists on their first experience in the forest, we measure the ambient comfort by the number

Fire, frost, and fur somehow coexist in this unreal suite at the Ice Hotel near Quebec City (above). The corridor, decorated with ice sculptures, leads to the entrance of the bar (facing page).

Despite the intense cold of the Saguenay region, the wood stove in the tent at the Aventure Mikuan II camp not only radiates welcome warmth, but also keeps essential items dry.

Gordon Moar, a trapper and the founder of Aventure Mikuan II. These moccasins and elk and caribou slippers were made by the trapper's mother, who also added the traditional embroidery.

of degrees over the freezing point. But the tent is much more comfortable than we could have imagined: the floor is covered with fir branches, a piece of canvas, a mattress, and, on top of all this, thick sleeping bags. The bitter cold wakes us up regularly throughout the night, just in time to drop another log into the small stove.

Gordon Moar, originally a Native Canadian trapper of Innu and Cree ancestry, created Aventure Mikuan II (pronounced may-koon, which means "feather" in the Innu language) in the 1990s to return to an ancestral way of life. The strong sixty-five-year-old proposes ecotourism adventures to visitors from Europe and Quebec, including an interpretation of the forest flora and fauna, summer and winter, in the Ashuapmushuan wildlife reserve, near Chibougamau in Saguenay. "I want people to know the reality, and I avoid folklore," he says. "We are modern, but that doesn't mean we don't talk about nature and our customs."

This reality is demonstrated through the practice of traditional techniques, such as the wooden snowshoes that are fashioned under his expert touch and the tool handles he makes from animal bones.

"Initially, the camp was extremely rudimentary, but people asked me not to change anything," says Moar. Nevertheless, over time, he installed bathrooms, which add considerable comfort, especially for long stays. The camp consists of a few tents and a log cabin, with living room and kitchen where everyone shares meals and the traditional bread, bannock. These group meals give us a chance to share our cultures.

Moar became a guide at the age of thirteen and knows the forest well. He teaches us orientation techniques for getting around the deep forests. "I look for the longest branches of the tree; they point south," he reveals. Nature is generous to those who understand it.

HERITAGE

Creativity, a reflection of the sensibilities and expertise of craftsmen, is a good expression of the art of living. An object beautifies everyday life, regardless of whether it is the result of an interpretation of reality, a product of the imagination, or a historical reconstructions. Various groups have been established, notably the Cercle des Fermières, an association of women who have been transmitting the culinary, cultural, and craft heritage of Quebec for eighty-five years. Other studio-companies (called economuseums*) also use traditional production techniques. Open to the public, they offer tours so that visitors can learn about their traditions; they also help to promote the value of the objects and the craftsmen. The first to join these companies was the Papeterie Saint-Gilles in Charlevoix.

Many creative companies combine tradition and modernism, such as the trendy furriers of Mariouche Gagné.

The reconstruction of a Huron village near Quebec City, Onhoüa Chetek8E, takes us back to the origins of this important nation. Two magnificent manor houses, the Manoir Mauvide-Genest and the Manoir Papineau, are rare illustrations of a distant, though still vibrant past. And the popularity of the famous Jardins de Métis in Grand-Métis on the Gaspé Peninsula speaks for the fondness of Quebeckers for horticulture.

PORTRAIT OF THE CRAFTSMEN

Being a craftsman is a true calling. For many years, the craftsman's status made him the poor relation of the creative arts. But the "profession" of craftsman has since acquired its own legitimacy. The quality and rigor of the work are now recognized, as is the contribution to an increasingly uniform society.

Wood. Canoes are commonplace in this immense land of lakes and rivers. Rapid and lightweight, they were always a favored mode of transportation for Native Canadians, as well as for trappers. The canoe plays an important role in a tale written by Honoré Beaugrand, "La Chasse-galerie," which was inspired by popular folklore from the trapper era: "With the first strokes of the paddle, the canoe launched into the air like an arrow, and the devil carried us away."

The woodworker Alain Rhéaume has transformed the humble canoe into a stylish work of art. This craftsman builds cedar boats that are described as Rolls-Royces and are sold throughout the world. The reputation of the native of Grandes Piles

The dream-catcher is a traditional talisman which protects dreamers from bad dreams; they are captured in the web and perish in the light of the day.

The historic general store at Anse-à-Beaufils was constructed in 1928 by Robin, Jones and Whitman Ltd., a powerful Anglo-Norman company from the Channel Islands. It is filled with woodwork, old books, objects, tools, and goods from days past. The storekeepers wear period costumes and recount the often difficult daily lives of the region's inhabitants. For years, the company maintained control over people's lives as both an employer and supplier, through a system of advances and exchanges.

In Alain Rhéaume's shop in Mauricie, the cedar ribs have been fitted and the cedar planking added, forming the canoe structure (above). Too small to be used on the water, these five-foot (1.5-meter) canoes often decorate shop fronts (right).

in La Mauricie (who also designs furniture) is due to the exceptional quality of the construction and the unrivaled finish. "I apprenticed alongside the great Belgian cabinetmaker Jules van Neste. He not only taught me to be confident in my techniques, but also awoke in me a love of wood," says Rhéaume. Indeed, his canoes reflect his love of elegant design and beautiful proportions.

He has been designing canoes since 1986, a step he feels was a natural process as a creator. "The canoe is a useful means of transportation, but our finishing techniques make them more beautiful," adds Rhéaume. His canoes are made of red cedar from British Columbia and white cedar from Quebec. Everything is done by hand: the strips of wood are steam-curved and assembled on a mold, which varies according to the owner's stated use; the planks are fitted; and the two thousand brass nails hand hammered into the boat. The long sanding process creates a smooth surface, an essential step before the several coats of marine varnish. This final process is critical, as it is this operation that gives the canoe its prized luster. He is one of the few canoe builders in North America, and his workshop produces twenty to twenty-five canoes a year, primarily for clients in the United States and Europe.

Weaving. France Hervieux, an excellent reference in terms of the traditional Québécois arrowhead sash, has been an avid weaver for fifteen years. The daughter of a textile merchant, France Hervieux was born in L'Assomption in Lanaudière, the cradle of traditional arrowhead sash production in Quebec. These sashes appeared in the nineteenth century; the women of L'Assomption were inspired by the arrival of rich Scottish merchants to produce and sell these popular fashion accessories. The Canadian settlers wore the wool sash with the herringbone motif, while the Scottish donned their tartans. It was only later that the design transformed into a zigzag, arrowhead pattern. "This development shows that they were seeking visual harmony and perfection. Textile specialists acknowledge that the arrowhead sash is the most beautiful finger-woven fabric in the world," explains the weaver.

The true arrowhead sash always has a red center, and the sequence of colors is invariable: a lightning bolt in white, then dark blue, then light blue, red, yellow, and finally green. The other strips that finish the sash may be of different colors, depending on the wool available. As opposed to a loom that uses warp and weft threads (as for the *catalogne*), the arrowhead sash is created from four hundred strands of wool, which are alternately used as warp and weft threads. This method produces a uniform design, and the sash has the same beautiful pattern on both sides. The texture is identical to that of older fibers, because the yarn is spun on a spinning-wheel to produce the desired texture. A sash represents some 350 hours of work and is a true collector's item. The usual way to wear the sash is to wind it twice around the waist and knot the fringe.

A traditional handmade arrowhead sash. Each of the four hundred strands of wool may be up to sixteen feet (five meters) long and are woven in a specific pattern of colors. Here, France Hervieux reproduces the characteristic lightning motif of the so-called "Assumption" sash, one of the two authentic designs (top). This beaded arrowhead sash by Éric Champagne de Berthier in Lanaudière represents the second type of design. This pattern was created by the First Nations peoples, who adapted the original design (bottom).

Braided rugs and quilts are not only practical, as they are made from recycled clothes and fabrics; they are also decorative. At Sainte-Rose-du-Nord in the Saguenay region, two craftswomen, members of the local Cercle des Fermières, create a number of accessories once commonly used in camps and log cabins. The authentic braided rug is handmade (top). This quilt, another vibrant local tradition, is an interpretation of the traditional "thousand pyramid" motif (bottom).

The *catalogne* appeared in Nouvelle France in the eighteenth century, and was one of the family's most precious possessions, carefully stored in wood chests. *Catalognes* are extremely warm bedcovers and have become contemporary items as they are made from strips of recycled cotton or wool cloths—often rags, sheets, and recycled clothing. A *catalogne* may be single-colored or have a pattern. They are also used as throw rugs. At the Cercle des Fermières of Saint-Fulgence in Saguenay, Yvonne Bélanger has been perpetuating the traditional *catalogne* weaving technique for two years. "The *catalogne* is a family heirloom, and for my children, it's an object that comes from their mother," she says. The strips are carefully assembled into a long strand that is then woven into the warp and weft on the loom. It takes a week or two to prepare the loom, a process that requires two weavers.

Braided rugs and quilts are also made from recycled material, but they are not woven. The first consists of strips of woven fabric, twisted in spirals, while the quilts use bits of fabric that are sewn together, lined and padded, and then quilted or sewn into patterns. They may have contemporary or traditional motifs, including the star of Bethlehem, a saw-tooth pattern or an Irish chain design. Quilts appeared in Quebec in the nineteenth century with the arrival of English immigrants in North America. The Eastern Townships region is well known for its magnificent quilts.

Fur. The country developed thanks to its fur trade. This fabulously warm and soft material has become highly controversial, but it is not really a luxury item in this climate. Furs are part of the collective Québécois unconscious. "It reminds me of childhood memories, New Year's Eve where we would roll ourselves up in our aunts' fur coats," remembers designer Mariouche Gagné. Yet ecology is central to the philosophy of her company Harricana, created in 1995 in Montreal. The Quebec native is the first to have marketed her designs of recycled furs. In 1994, when she was a student at the prestigious Domus Academy in Milan, Mariouche Gagné participated in a competition launched by the Conseil Canadien de la Fourrure. She came up with the idea of using one of her mother's old fur coats for her design submitted to the competition.

Nearly six thousand fur coats, still in good condition, are recycled every year. The furs are examined carefully for any trace of dryness or mildew. They are then taken apart, re-cut and transformed into one-of-a-kind pieces. Six years ago, sensing the upcoming cocooning trend, she added household items to her ready-to-wear collection: luxury accessories, including fabulous cushions and blankets. Fur is a perfect material for innovation. Harricana now sells superb woven fur blankets that are amazingly light and soft.

The cotton fibers are pressed and placed on a screen to form the handmade paper produced by the Papeterie Saint-Gilles, situated near Quebec City. The sheets are stacked between two thick layers of felt, which are placed in a hydraulic press to remove the water, and then suspended and dried in the open air for at least twenty-four hours (left). At designer Mariouche Gagné's Montreal company, Harricana, an old fur coat is transformed into an item of clothing or luxury accessory for the home (right).

Handmade paper. The Papeterie Saint-Gilles was founded in 1965 by Monseigneur Félix-Antoine Savard who is, among other occupations, a horticulturist, a poet, and a novelist. His aim was to revive the traditional handmade paper production from the eighteenth century. The workshop in the former village school of Saint-Joseph-de-la-Rive in Charlevoix produces luxury paper made of pure cotton rag in ecru, white, and ivory tones used for "quality" correspondence, silkscreen printing, and fine book-binding. The warm, soft texture of the Saint-Gilles mottled papers offers a wonderful creative medium. "A sheet of paper is not used only for writing. It can also serve to make any number of decorative objects," explains the company director Hélène Desgagnés, a master papermaker for eighteen years. She has used Saint-Gilles paper to create astonishing pieces of jewelry, decorative boxes, and original screens. The workshop produces 60,000 to 90,000 sheets of paper per year. Some include maple leaves, ferns, or even strands of hemp. But the delicate flower petals of the spiked pur-ple loosestrife and hawkweed on the paper are the shop's trademark.

The Manoir Mauvide-Genest on Île d'Orléans is a rare example of a French-style manor house from the eighteenth century (above). The site of Onhoüa Chetek8E, also near Quebec City, offers an overview of the life of the Hurons; here, the longhouse, where the clan lived (facing page).

ARCHITECTURAL HERITAGE

Books often recreate the past and its traditions. In Quebec, where the motto is "Je me souviens" (I remember), memory is preserved in a number of museums, like the Musée de la Civilisation in Quebec City and the Musée McCord in Montreal, as well as in the architecture of theme villages scattered throughout the territory. One such place is the Village Québécois d'Antan in Drummondville in the St. Lawrence Plain, a reconstruction of nineteenth-century life.

Visitors to the Manoir Mauvide-Genest are amazed to discover the life of Jean Mauvide, a surgeon who became a squire and lived the good life on the Île d'Orléans, a place seemingly forgotten by time. An analysis of the paint layers on the manor's walls helped restorers recreate the brilliant eighteenth-century colors. Historical documents, as well as the oral histories of Hurons, also helped illuminate the simple and elegant lifestyle of that time, visible at the village of Onhoüa Chetek8E.

The reconstruction at the Manoir Papineau was greatly facilitated by the abundant correspondence between members of the Papineau family. Period photographs reveal the elegant and even elaborate decoration. Photography also provided a crucial contribution for the Jardins de Métis. Over ten thousand photographs, all imbued with a love of nature and tasteful civility, capture the ambiance of another age at Villa Reford.

A Huron village: Onhoüa Chetek8E

We are at Wendake, a few miles from Quebec City. Our guide François Dubois greets us at Onhoüa Chetek8E, which means "from yesterday to today," in the Huron language. The recreated village includes traditional buildings, a vegetable garden, ancestral medicine, and traditional rites, presenting an authentic look at a fascinating way of life. We start the visit at the longhouse, the hub of the village, where women made the important decisions. In this matrilineal society, the women oversaw the social life and needs of the clan, and also took care of education and ensuring respect for traditions. It was a democratic and open society geared toward sharing.

Life in the village revolved around the longhouse, a large wooden structure covered with birch bark. Several generations from the same clan worked in various areas, each of which had a specific purpose: food preparation, food conservation, and the production of clothing and everyday objects. Comfort was essential. The two-level sleeping platforms for families provided living space below and storage room above. Fires built directly on the packed earth provided warmth. They were used as cooking fires but also as a heat source, as stones were packed under and around the fire. The rounded roof, nearly thirty feet (nine meters) high, often had a smoke hole. Meals were prepared twice a day, and the entire family gathered together around the fires.

The Hurons also like the sweat lodge, an oval wooden structure covered with leather or bark. It was used for physical and spiritual purification. We learn about medicinal plants and also discover that decoctions of tree bark provided many useful remedies. Willow bark, for example, contains salicylic acid, a natural aspirin. Appearances were also extremely important; the Hurons liked to look attractive, smoothing their hair with sunflower oil and wearing beaded leather clothes. This concern for beauty extended to everyday objects and traditional rituals, such as the production of elegantly simple ceramics and bark baskets. They are beautiful expressions of a harmonious mode of life.

An eighteenth-century manor on the Île d'Orléans: Manoir Mauvide-Genest

The Île d'Orléans is only a few miles from Quebec City, linked to the northern shore of the St. Lawrence River by a single bridge. The original structure of Manoir Mauvide-Genest, located at Saint-Jean-de-l'Île-d'Orléans, was constructed during the reign of Louis XV and is a beautiful example of the manor houses built in the eighteenth century in rural environments. The owner, Jean Mauvide, was a young French surgeon who married a village woman in 1733 and constructed his home in 1734. He became the squire and transformed his home into a manor house in 1752. Now completely restored, this imposing four-floor building (including a large basement and an attic) reflects the status and prosperity of the residents.

From the entrance, a series of rooms offer a magnificent view of the brightly lit ground floor. We had imagined that the spaces would be austere. They are, instead, comfortable and cheery, with a preference for stripes and prints, a fashion of the period. The small sitting room, next to the study, is anything but monotonous, decorated in bright yellow and turquoise. The dining room was designed to accommodate large receptions and features limewood floors and ocher, orange, and mocha walls. The adjacent kitchen is furnished with rustic wood furniture, which matches the beams, pine floors, and stone fireplace. Upstairs, a large corridor leads to six rooms, which have connecting doors. Gold and dark green form the overall color scheme.

A few pieces of period furniture and objects still remain, including the lovely "capucine" chairs in the kitchen and a loom in one of the bedrooms. For the rest, the interior decoration is a recreation, based on engravings by Jean Siméon Chardin illustrating eighteenth-century life. Most of the decorative objects come from museums.

Manoir Mauvide-Genest introduces us to a pleasant way of life, with the minimal acceptable dose of religion both for Jean Mauvide and the rest of the inhabitants of the island, according to the director Claire Rémillard. This rural lifestyle appealed so much to the English conquerors in 1760 that they hesitated many long years before changing one iota.

This room in the Manoir Mauvide-Genest on the Île d'Orléans was used for the patients of the surgeon/squire (facing page). A traditional folding table and chair from the Île d'Orléans (above).

P for Patrie (homeland), symbol of the Société Saint-Jean-Baptiste in 1864; the maple leaf and the beaver also symbolize Canada (right).

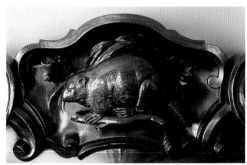

Near the Ottawa River in Montebello stands the Normandy-inspired Manoir Papineau. It is flanked by two towers; the one with several windows was used as a greenhouse.

Manoir Papineau at Montebello, in the French medieval style

In Quebec, the expression "to have a Papineau head," means to be intelligent. The expression refers to the brilliant politician and scholar Louis-Joseph Papineau. The residence we are visiting has as many contrasts as did the major figure who lived here. He believed that the manorial regime was essential to the survival of the French-Canadian identity, although he openly admired American democracy.

Constructed in the late nineteenth century on the banks of the Ottawa River at Montebello in the Ottawa region, the Louis-Joseph Papineau manor house was modeled after the French medieval château. It features a Regency-style façade, characteristic of nineteenth-century homes. The structure was also influenced by the Pittoresque style, an American import that stressed the relationship between the individual and nature. At the time it was built, the property was immense, nearly fifteen miles (twenty-five kilometers) in circumference, with meadows, groves, vegetable gardens, and orchards. Today, a driveway winds through a large park and outbuildings before reaching the museum. On arrival, we are immediately directed toward one of the four towers. A magnificent spiral staircase leads to the upper floors. The ground floor, the "noble floor," has a large, luminous corridor. In the autumn, stoves and pipes were installed here to heat the household. The corridor separates the small sitting room, the master bedroom, the two girls' rooms, the dining room, and the large yellow living room. Just to the right of the entrance is a small sitting room that leads to the master bedroom. The patina of the wood paneling in this bedroom, along with a whimsical Rococo mirror and Provencal fabric, adds a warm touch to the somewhat austere room. Upstairs are the original seven rooms: six guest rooms and a study.

The corridor continues to the dining room and the small office, then to the yellow living room, the only place that still has the original tapestries, which have been carefully restored, and to the blue sitting room. Almost all the furniture and decorative objects in the richly decorated yellow room are original, gifts from the Papineau family. This is where the immediate family gathered, along with guests, friends, members of the omnipresent clergy, and fellow politicians.

In the bedroom of the politician Louis-Joseph Papineau, the beaver fur hat sits awaiting its owner (below).

Original decorative objects and furniture from the yellow sitting room in the Manoir Papineau in Montebello. The chandelier, tapestry, and seating reflect the exuberant Victorian style.

NATURAL BEAUTY

The landscapes in the heart of this sparsely populated land offer a multitude of new discoveries, even for Quebeckers. The state organization alone, the Sociéte des Établissements de Plein Air du Québec, includes a network of twenty-two national parks, sixteen reserves, and eighteen tourist centers. These are fairly staggering numbers, without counting the many sites created by private initiative. These include the Grands Jardins de Normandin in the Lac Saint-Jean region, which offers an overview of the art of gardening. There are also collective initiatives. Les Amis des Jardins, a not-for-profit organization in Métis on the Gaspé Peninsula, promotes and preserves unique gardens.

A horticultural wonder: the Jardins de Métis and Villa Reford

The Jardins de Métis in Grand-Métis on the Gaspé Peninsula are among the most beautiful in Canada. Situated on the confluent of the Mitis River and the St. Lawrence River, they are part of the large property that used to be called Estevan Lodge, then Villa Redford. They were created as a series of basins forming a point toward the river. The proximity of the river and the layout protect the gardens from the harsh *nordet** wind, creating an exceptional microclimate. It is a rich floral museum, created by the self-taught horticulturist Elsie Reford. During her many travels abroad, she loved to bring back rare plants, including the Himalayan blue poppy. This garden was created differently from the traditional large garden, which often involved major transformations of the natural setting. Rather than hire a landscape designer, as was the custom at the time, the avant-garde gardener did everything herself. And rather than make nature conform to her designs, she fully integrated the "exoticism" of the local species. Created from 1920 to 1959 during family holidays, the sixteen thematic gardens contain more than three thousand plant species and varieties. The spirit of Elsie Reford hovers over the gardens to this day, in the predominantly blue and pink flowers. Between a hundred and two hundred and fifty plants and flowers are planted every year. A new addition, a welcome garden, has recently added "Explorateurs" roses, which are hardy Canadian hybrids with vibrant, deep pink blossoms. The spirit of the place, entirely devoted to the serenity desired by the original gardener, has been preserved. Indeed, Alexander Reford, her great-grandson and director of the gardens, says: "I think we need to avoid being excessive. Beauty lies in eliminating the unnecessary. The rhythm of the transitions is very important; the empty spaces must be followed by richly colored areas." As in theater and life itself, intense moments exist alongside more reflective ones. The Belvedere, facing the river, has not been renovated. It remains a place of contemplation, as the role of the surrounding landscape is to sometimes surpass the floral beauty of the gardens.

The Jardins de Métis in Grand Métis, in the Appalachian region, offer a magnificent panorama. Begonias and crabapple trees grow among the azaleas (facing page). The porch of the imposing Villa Reford (the former Villa Estevan) in the Jardins de Métis is a lovely place to contemplate the luxurious vegetation (top). Elsie Reford was a self-taught gardener; she created these romantic gardens, including the small bridge that crosses the Page stream (bottom).

Maple syrup is excellent for breakfast, poured over pancakes. The syrup may be light, medium, or dark in color.

CULINARY HERITAGE

Let's explore the countless culinary pleasures on offer in Quebec, where many traditions still survive. It's hard not to see a parallel between the architectural diversity and the multiple influences in Québécois gastronomy. These various culinary contributions have resulted in a cuisine that is unique in the world. Quebeckers do not live in isolation, and they willingly return from trips abroad with all kinds of new ideas. There are imported goods, of course, but the constant need to innovate has created a mass of new, high-quality local products.

The contribution of native culture is immeasurable. Without it, the first French settlers would not have survived the harsh weather conditions. In terms of food, for example, they adopted products they had never seen before. The cranberry is a wonderful berry that grows wild along the coast and in peat bogs; this cousin of the blueberry is a rich source of vitamin C. Wild rice is also gathered in the wetlands; this is not actually rice, but an aquatic grass, *zizania aquatica*. Native Canadians used *zizania*, a natural thickener, in their hearty soups. It was also served as rice, as a side dish to game. Corn is a big favorite in Quebec, and is a staple in the Native Canadian diet. First Nations peoples originally prepared corn by placing the corncobs directly on the fire. Now, of course, everyone eats boiled corn smothered in butter and salt. Fresh corn is one of the big treats of any late-summer meal.

The First Nations also taught the settlers about maple sap and how to make a number of products from it, including the famous syrup. This was a major discovery for Quebeckers, who instantly loved the sweet syrup. As for the Irish, they shared the recipe for their stew, a simple yet delicious dish prepared in the autumn, consisting of beef and root vegetables. Traditional Québécois cuisine and Russian cuisine have similarities; they both use marinades and salt to conserve food, and have a strong preference for pork, potatoes, cabbage, and turnips. Québécois cuisine changes rapidly, but it has retained its French origins, such as the *tourtière* from Lac Saint-Jean, which is an exact replica of a French meat pie called a *berrichonne*.

Québécois hospitality also appears in a wide range of flavors: there are routes devoted to wine, cheese, special products, along which are a number of rural restaurants well worth exploring. Each region has its own specialties. Game, for example, is king in the heart of the Abitibi, as are the freshwater fish such as the *ouananiche* and the *muskellunge**. The Laurentians are best known for fruits and vegetables. The Appalachians, along the southern bank of the St. Lawrence River, is the place to find pheasants and guinea fowls; the duck from Lac Brome in the Eastern Townships is widely acclaimed. You can also find cheese, including the delicious Lechevalier Maillous.

The Gaspé Peninsula favors a fish and shellfish cuisine. The lobster, the giant scallop, the blue mussel, and the famous Pied-de-Vent, a soft-curd, raw milk cheese, are the specialties of the Îles de la Madeleine. Food here is simple and hearty; the *pot-en-pot*, a specialty, consists of potatoes and seafood baked in a pastry, like a meat pie.

The coast offers surprising discoveries: the Charlevoix region is famous for its veal, lamb, and mutton. The pasturelands along the banks of the St. Lawrence River give the meat its prized salty flavor. The region also produces several great cheeses, which have become famous, including the delicious semisoft Migneron, which blends the flavors of walnut, butter, and a touch of salt. The multiethnic city of Montreal is a microcosm of international gastronomy. In addition, it has its own specialties, including smoked meat on rye bread, and bagels.

From top to bottom, left to right: Trout served with corn and wild rice, a grain gathered in wetlands. Traditional First Nations bread. Fruit ketchup, beets, and pickles. Meatball stew. Soufflé omelet. Corn on the cob. Above, right: Cornflour pancakes and beans, a nourishing traditional First Nations dish.

The Gaspé Peninsula is famous for lobster, especially as served at the Capitaine Homard restaurant in Sainte-Flavie (top left). This aggressive and delicious crustacean is the subject of elaborate compositions in the restaurant's dining room. The acclaimed Maison du Pêcheur restaurant in Percé on the Gaspé Peninsula also serves lobster; diners can sample the simple and refined local specialties, notably the mussels and lobster with butter (bottom left). The Quebec Lobster Festival starts in June.

Beer is the national drink in Quebec. The first brewery opened in 1647 in Quebec City, followed by another in Montreal in 1786. For several years now, the trend has been toward specialty beers produced by microbreweries. Some of these refreshing and delicious light, dark, or red brews are named after the numerous tales and legends of Quebec.

As opposed to the wide choice and high quality of the beer and cheese (which has been produced for over one hundred years in Quebec), winemaking is a more recent industry. It began in the 1980s, but vintners have succeeded in producing high-quality wines, particularly specialty wines. The Eastern Townships is a major wine-producing region, with a large concentration of vine-growers in Dunham. The harsh climate is put to good use here, with the creation of an ice wine*.

Apples, a specialty of the Montérégie region, are also processed to make cider. Once disparaged, cider is now considered an elegant beverage that is the subject of specialized tastings. Liqueurs are also highly prized. The cloudberry* or salmonberry grows on the North Shore; it is a type of wild blackberry that is made into an exquisite sweet-and-sour liqueur.

Traditional dishes generally come from hearty family-style cooking. Indeed, farmers and lumberjacks needed to eat well to have enough energy to work outdoors in the rugged climate. Inevitably, this traditional fare was gradually relegated to family meals during holidays, notably Christmas and New Year's Eve. Lighter versions have appeared alongside the traditional meal. Both are extremely popular these days.

At the sugarhouse of the Sucrerie de la Montagne, situated in Rigaud, Montérégie, the cuisine is an explosion of Québécois candor and joie de vivre. Visitors here carouse to traditional music and sing-alongs, in an ambience described by owner Pierre Faucher as "the good old times." All the dishes come from his mother's collection of family recipes: the *tourtières*, beans and bacon, meatball stew and pigs' feet, maple-smoked ham, and a soufflé omelet. The tables always have the ubiquitous bottle of maple syrup, produced right here. The fruit ketchup (which includes peaches, pears, celery, onions, and tomatoes, among other ingredients) is a sheer delight, appreciated by both Québécois visitors and foreigners. Broiled meat is another specialty here, notably maple-smoked pork and bison.

Aux Anciens Canadiens, a restaurant located in the oldest house in Quebec City (1675), brings the seventeenth century back to life. This establishment has windows with small panes, thick wainscoted walls, and low ceilings. The menu offers a traditional pea soup, bean soup, the Lac Saint-Jean *tourtière*, and a maple syrup tart. You'll love the simplicity and sweet treat of a traditional snack: farmhouse bread with maple syrup and cream. The menu changes regularly and features Québécois nouvelle cuisine, which combines popular products such as caribou, deer, and elk with diverse local traditions.

The food culture is extremely dynamic in Quebec, which offers a number of interesting gastronomical tastes. Fiddleheads (the coiled tips of young fern fronds), for example, are gathered in early summer, and are delicious served with vinaigrette.

Rising young chefs also promote the products of local farmers and regional items, by creating innovative and colorful new dishes. The current trend is toward a market cuisine that focuses on fresh products. In the summer, they use small summer fruits and new carrots; in the autumn, pumpkin and squash. Root vegetables appear on the winter menu, notably parsley root, which is more flavorful than salsify (oyster plant). Within this maelstrom of culinary creativity, traditional cuisine has been revamped and is now more avant-garde. Québécois chefs have constantly strived to perfect innovative cuisine.

Beer is the national drink, the stuff of tales and legends, and an inseparable part of Québécois tradition. The names are evocative: La Maudite (the accursed) and Eau Bénite (holy water) (top). Dunham, in Eastern Townships in the Appalachians, offers many chances to sample the high-quality local wines, such as Blancs Coteaux (bottom). The owner of the Sucrerie de la Montagne in Rigaud, in the St. Lawrence Plain, carefully tends his stove (following pages).

USEFUL INFORMATION

Quebec has so much to offer that it is impossible to list everything here. In addition to the places mentioned or illustrated in the Rendezvous chapter, this section presents other sites of interest for a more varied itinerary. Some of the establishments in regional areas function as inns, art galleries, and cafés all rolled into one. This feature adds depth to the local color. In terms of shopping, it's possible to find unique items in the department stores, but you're far more likely to pick up something unusual in small specialized shops.

WHAT TO SEE

This chapter is divided into ten sections, classified by category and region. The addresses are listed in alphabetical order. The websites at the end of this chapter are good sources for additional tourist information. The site of the Société des établissements de plein air du Québec (SEPAQ) includes relevant information concerning the national parks, reserves, and holiday centers in the region.

To telephone Quebec from the United States, dial 1 followed by the area code (in parentheses) and the seven-digit telephone number; to telephone from the United Kingdom, dial 001 followed by the area code and seven-digit number.

APPALACHIANS

(Eastern Townships-Gaspé Peninsula)

ORFORD ART CENTRE

3165, chemin du Parc, route 141 Nord
Orford, PQ
Canada J1X 7A2
Tel: (819) 843-9871/843-3981
Fax: (819) 843-7274
centre@arts-orford.org
The Orford Art Centre, situated within the Parc National du Mont Orford, offers a classical music and visual arts program. Every year, the internationally acclaimed music academy hosts students from around the world who come here to take master classes with musicians such as Anton Kuerti and Marc Durand. These students also perform in public during summer concerts. The center also has three major exhibitions per year featuring contemporary, lyric, or figurative works by Quebec artists. Visitors are welcome to explore the Arts Trail, a path featuring modern stone, wood, and metal sculptures, for an unforgettable visual experience.

LAURENTIANS

LE PATRIOTE THEATER

258, rue Saint-Venant
Sainte-Agathe-des-Monts, PQ
Canada J8C 3K6
Tel: (819) 326-3655
Fax: (819) 326-7196
info@theatrepatriote.com
One of the oldest and most popular summer theaters in Quebec.

MONTREAL

CENTRE CANADIEN D'ARCHITECTURE (CCA)

1920, rue Baile
Montreal, PQ
Canada H3H 2S6
Tel: (514) 939-7026
A major international research center and a venue for large-scale events and exhibitions.

EX-CENTRIS

3536, bd Saint-Laurent
Montreal, PQ
Canada H2X 2V1
Tel: (514) 847-3536
Fax: (514) 847-0966
info@ex-centris.com
Montreal's avant-garde film scene makes its home at the Ex-Centre complex. It houses among other things three public theaters that show independent movies. The Parallèle, Fellini, and Cassavetes theaters each have their own programming: the Parallèle projects art films and videos, while the Fellini shows feature films and also doubles as an exhibition space.

MONUMENT NATIONAL

1182, bd Saint-Laurent
Montreal, PQ
Canada H2X 2S5
Tel: (514) 871-2224
Fax: (514) 871-8298
info@monument-national.qc.ca
A Montreal institution, constructed in 1893, which was restored to its former splendor in 1993. The Monument National is a dance, opera, and theater space, as well as a springboard for graduates of the National Theatre School. Special events are also held here.

PLACE DES ARTS

260, bd de Maisonneuve
Montreal, PQ
Canada H2X 1Y9
Tel: (514) 285-2112
billets@pda.qc.ca
This complex includes five performance halls, notably for symphonic concerts and plays. The esplanade is used for annual festivals such as the Montreal International Jazz Festival.

THÉÂTRE DU NOUVEAU MONDE

84, rue Sainte-Catherine Ouest
Montreal, PQ
Canada H2X 1Z6
Tel: (514) 878-7878
Fax: (514) 878-7880
info@tnm.qc.ca
The only theater in North America that still has a hall with symmetrical proportions (a perfect cube, as with Italian-style theaters). The current establishment performs a repertory of classical and contemporary pieces, with many first-run creations. The Café du Nouveau Monde, in the same building, is a lively artistic haunt.

North

Abitibi
Rouyn-Noranda

Témiscamingue

Ottawa River

ONTARIO

Gatin

0   200 km

Map: **Édigraphie**, Rouen 2004

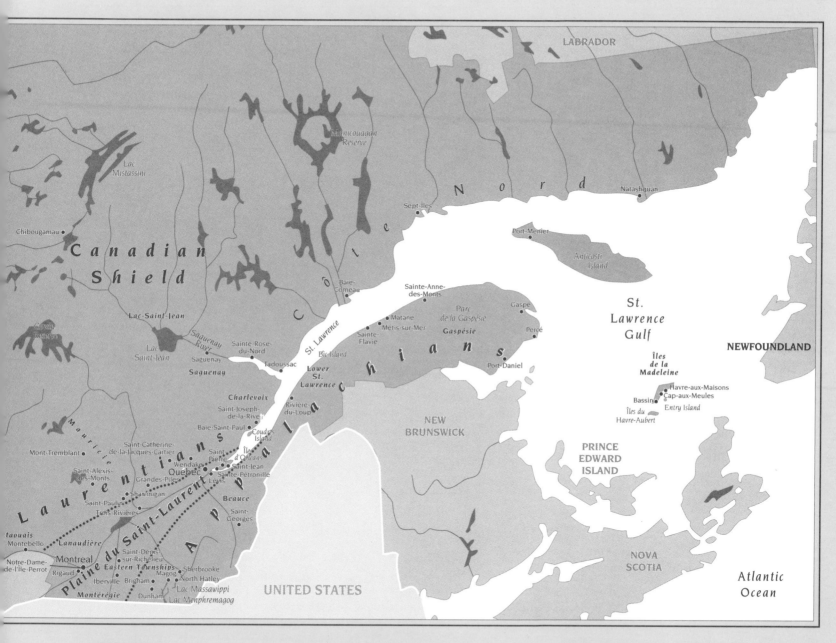

QUEBEC CITY AND REGION

HÔTEL DU PARLEMENT

1045, bd des Parlementaires
Quebec, PQ
Canada G1A 1A3

Tel: (418) 643-7239
Constructed between 1877 and 1886, the Second Empire structure is the seat of the National Assembly. At nightfall, the building's main façade is illuminated.

QUEBEC CITY OBSERVATORY

Édifice Marie-Guyart
1037, rue de la Chevrotière, 31ᵉ étage
Quebec, PQ
Canada G1R 5E9

Tel: (418) 644-9841
Fax: (418) 644-2879
info@observatoirecapitale.org
Situated at an altitude of 711 feet (221 meters), the top of this structure offers a spectacular view over the city.

The observatory is also a center for the city's history and the starting point for thematic hikes that allow visitors to trace the military, religious, and architectural heritage of the provincial capital.

ANTIQUE DEALERS AND ART GALLERIES

APPALACHIANS

(Eastern Townships-Gaspé Peninsula)

CENTRE D'ART
MARCEL GAGNON
564, route de la Mer
Sainte-Flavie, PQ
Canada G0J 2L0
Tel: (418) 775-2829
Fax: (418) 775-9548
info@centredart.net
This inn, restaurant, and art gallery is open from early May to mid-October. The center exhibits unusual sculptures emerging from the St. Lawrence River. Entitled *Le Grand Rassemblement*, the work by Marcel Gagnon represents a procession of figures made of reinforced concrete moving toward and disappearing into the sea. The sculptures, like the paintings, are naive in style.

MAISONART
826, route 132, C.P. 216
Anse-à-Beaufils
Percé, PQ
Canada G0C 2L0
Tel. and Fax:
(418) 782-2047
maisonar@globetrotter.net
John Wiseman was born in the province of Ontario, where he was a biologist and illustrator for the Canadian Wildlife Service, before becoming a professional painter. He moved to Percé in 1975. The Gaspé Peninsula scenery and the wildlife provide an endless source of inspiration. He has become internationally famous for the energetic expressive style and delicate lines of his watercolors of animals (notably the eagle owl) in their natural habitat.

LOWER ST. LAWRENCE

GALERIE DU BIC
191, rue Sainte-Cécile
Le Bic, PQ
Canada G0L 1B0
Tel: (418) 736-5113
galerie@galeriedubic.com
Outside are the enchanting islands of Bic. Inside the century-old restored home are the impressive works of professional Québécois painters. These artists are part of a group of friends who have been meeting together for twenty-five years to paint landscapes of the region. One of them, Guy Legaré, created the gallery to provide a place where they could all exhibit their works.

ÎLES DE LA MADELEINE

LE VENT
DANS LES TOILES
(by appointment)
Tel: (418) 986-6558
(studio)
(418) 989-9274 (boutique)
mb@leventdanslestoiles.com
This painter expresses his personal and contemporary approach through mixed techniques, notably oil, engraving, and image transfer.

LAURENTIANS

S. TRÉPANIER & FILS
ANTIQUES
670, bd des Laurentides
(route 117)
Piedmont, PQ
Canada J0R 1K0
Tel: (450) 227-3532
Fax: (450) 227-7153
danielle.thibault@sympatico.ca
Authentic Canadian memorabilia, including antique Québécois furniture and folk art.

GALERIE
LE CASTELET
4, rue Filion
Saint-Sauveur-des-Monts, PQ
Canada J0R 1R0
Tel: (450) 227-9797
Fax: (450) 227-7855
info@galerielecastelet.ca
This art gallery exhibits well-known Québécois artists, including René Richard, as well as new artists. It shows contemporary, naive, and figurative works, among other styles.

MONTREAL

ALTERNA-TIF
122, rue Bernard Ouest
Montreal, PQ
Canada H2T 2K1
Tel: (514) 948-3573
Fax: (514) 948-1547
salon_alternatif@videotron.ca
This unique avant-garde site, situated in the Mile End neighborhood, offers contemporary art, design, and the latest in trendy haircuts.

BUTIN
3411, rue Sainte-Catherine Est
Montreal, PQ
Canada H1W 2E1
Tel: (514) 523-2138
pierre_plante@sympatico.ca
A brilliant shop with colorful walls where you can find traditional wooden toys, stained-glass windows, decorative accessories and objects, nineteenth- and twentieth-century antique furniture, and reproductions. The owner, Pierre Plante, clearly loves to recreate the interiors that form a backdrop for his rare finds, like Portneuf dishes, porcelain specially made for Quebec in England starting in 1760.

GALA
5157, bd Saint-Laurent
Montreal, PQ
Canada H2T 1R9
Tel: (514) 279-4247
Fax: (514) 279-5367
gala@qc.aira.com
This gallery situated in the fashionable Mile End neighborhood exhibits powerful and original artworks from this region and much further afield.

GALERIE SIMON
BLAIS
5420, bd Saint-Laurent, bureau 100
Montreal, PQ
Canada H2T 1S1
Tel: (514) 849-1165
Fax: (514) 849-1862
gal.simonblais@biz.videotron.ca
This large gallery is not only a showcase for works by major contemporary Canadian painters and sculptors, it is also a springboard for up-and-coming abstract and figurative painters.

QUEBEC CITY AND REGION

CENTRE D'ART DE
BAIE-SAINT-PAUL
4, rue Ambroise Fafard
Baie-Saint-Paul, PQ
Canada G3Z 2J2
Tel: (418) 435-5654
Fax: (418) 435-6269
The center includes studios, a shop, galleries, and exhibitions and hosts the reputed International Contemporary Art Symposium of Baie-Saint-Paul.

GALERIE
MADELEINE
LACERTE
1, côte Dinan
Quebec, PQ
Canada G1K 3V5
Tel: (418) 692-1566
Fax: (418) 692-4305
info@galerielacerte.com

ARCHITECTS, INTERIOR DESIGNERS, AND DECORATORS

One of the most important contemporary art galleries in Quebec. The gallery exhibits major international and Quebecois artists such as Marcele Ferron and the Lausanne artist Francine Simonin.

GALERIE ROUJE
228, rue Saint-Joseph Est
Quebec, PQ
Canada G1K 3A9
Tel: (418) 688-4777
rouje@bellnet.ca
The contemporary gallery and bar also exhibits foreign and Québécois visual artists.

MARCHÉ BONSECOURS

350, rue Saint-Paul Est
Montreal, PQ
Canada H2Y 1H2
Tel: (514) 872-7730
Fax: (514) 872-8477
This historic building in the heart of Old Montreal includes studios, shops, and art galleries:

BOUTIQUE BIJOUX
MÉTIERS D'ART
ET LES MÉTIERS
D'ART DE LA TABLE
Tel: (514) 878-2787
A shop selling craftwork by members of the Conseil des Métiers d'Art du Québec, notably whimsical jewelry with precious stones by Claudio Pino. There is also a large selection of table-

ware and decorative objects, such as creative tea (and coffee) sets by the ceramicist Géraldine Sempol and one-of-a-kind resin pieces by craftsman-designer Julia Asimakopulos

GALERIE DE
L'INSTITUT DE
DESIGN MONTRÉAL
(IDM)
Tel: (514) 866-2436, ext. 21
Fax: (514) 866-0881
The Galerie de l'IDM (actually a shop) is a showcase for Québécois industrial design, offering, among other objects, a plastic case by designer Michel Dallaire, who was hugely successful

LAURENTIANS

PASCALE GIRARDIN
(by appointment)
Tel: (450) 227-7585
Fax: (450) 227-0519
pascale.girardin@sympatico.ca
Architectural ceramics and marvelous contemporary creations for the home.

XTIAN DESIGN
(by appointment)
Tel: (450) 226-0044
Fax: (450) 226-1734
info@xtiandesign.com
Decorative objects, useful

accessories, and unusual furniture. Works with clean, poetic lines.

MONTREAL

BONALDO
407, bd Saint-Laurent
Montreal, PQ
Canada H2Y 2Y5
Tel: (514) 287-9222
Fax: (514) 287-7674
info@bonaldo.ca
Louis Bauzé's trendy boutique. This lovely, luminous space presents contemporary Italian designers in a relaxed setting.

in the 1990s, and the trendy "Flex" and "Fleur" tables by designer Michael Santella.

GOGO GLASS
(Studio-shop)
Tel: (514) 397-8882/878-9698
Sensational objects by Annie Michaud, such as the suggestive shapes and bright colors of the blown-glass citrus press.

MEUBLES
D'AUTREFOIS M.B.
Tel: (514) 875-4511
This establishment sells fine reproductions of eighteenth-century Québécois furniture.

DESIGNWORKS
(by appointment)
Tel: (514) 973-5140
Fax: (450) 442-4016
beroud_design@hotmail.com
Stainless steel objects and furniture by designer François Béroud.

ESPACE PEPIN
350, rue Saint-Paul Ouest
Montreal, PQ
Canada H2Y 2A6
Tel: (514) 844-0114
Fax: (514) 844-9714
art@pepart.com
This hybrid space recreates cozy interior settings; it's a concept apartment that showcases the immense acrylic canvases of the artist and owner Lysanne Pepin. Her nudes, horses, and still lifes hang alongside high-end furniture, contemporary decorative accessories, and vintage clothing.

HARRICANA
3000, rue Saint-Antoine Ouest
Montreal, PQ
Canada H4C 1A5
Tel: (514) 287-6517
Fax: (514) 287-7418
harricana@sprint.ca
Designer Mariouche Gagné's workshop/boutique. The immaculate space evokes the cold purity of icebergs, although the items are all soft, warm, and sensual. Furs, skins, and wool are recycled and transformed into terrific ready-to-wear

items that combine luxury, an outdoors feel, and originality.

IL N'Y A QUE DEUX
1405, rue Crescent
Montreal, PQ
Canada H3G 2B2
Tel: (514) 843-5665
Fax: (514) 843-9771
info@ilnyaquedeux.com
The elegance of Montreal ready-to-wear. The cuts and sober colors—with the exception of red, the shop's signature color—are showcased in an interior of steel, concrete, and stone created by interior designer Taras Iwanycki.

JEAN-CLAUDE
POITRAS
(by appointment)
Tel: (514) 906-1990
Fax: (514) 906-1989
jean-claude.poitras@mks.net
The renowned Montreal clothes designer divides his time between fashion, design, and interior decorating, along with his collection 13, at rue de l'Univers, dedicated to tableware.

M0851
3981, bd Saint-Laurent
Montreal, PQ
Canada H2W 1Y5
Tel: (514) 849-9759
Urban designs for the individual and the home. This Montreal designer (and manufacturer) offers bags, accessories, and clothes for

men and women. M0851 also designs furniture with comfort as a priority.

MODERNO
4268, bd Saint-Laurent
Montreal, PQ
Canada H2W 1Z3
Tel: (514) 842-4061
Fax: (514) 842-9084
info@modernofurniture.com
Montreal "ready-to-live" design, with collections of sofas, beds, chairs, and tables with pared-down lines.

MONTAUK
4404, bd Saint-Laurent
Montreal, PQ
Canada H2W 1Z5
Tel: (514) 845-8285
info@montauksofa.com
The trademark of this shop is its big, overstuffed sofas.

QUEBEC CITY AND REGION

BALTAZAR
461, rue Saint-Joseph Est
Quebec, PQ

Canada G1K 3B6
Tel: (418) 524-1991
Fax: (418) 524-1932
Urban furnishings and accessories for the home, with, among other items, Bidule, a collection of original salt and pepper mills.

BOUTIQUE MÉTIERS D'ART
29, rue Notre-Dame
Quebec, PQ
Canada G1K 4E9
Tel: (418) 694-0267

Fax: (418) 692-4271
cmaqque@total.net
The Conseil des Métiers d'Art du Québec has a shop in Montreal and in Quebec City, on Place Royale. In Quebec City, you can find small wooden boxes by Alain Talbot, utilitarian *raku* objects called Gigouilles by artist Gilles Belley, and landscapes of Quebec City on silk by Louis Lubuis—all regional members of the Conseil.

MÂ
261, rue Saint-Anselme
Quebec, PQ
Canada G1K 5S2
Tel: (418) 521-6262
Fax: (418) 521-7337
The Saint-Roch neighborhood in Quebec City has a large number of studios, contemporary design shops, and art galleries. Mâ proposes contemporary and antique Asian furniture. The shop also designs its own furniture.

CRAFTSMEN

ÎLES DE LA MADELEINE

ARTISANS DU SABLE
907, route 199, La Grave
C.P. 336
Havre-Aubert, PQ
Canada G0B 1J0
Tel.: (418) 937-2917
Fax: (418) 937-2129
info@artisansdusable.com
Sand-castles are anything but ephemeral on the islands. In this studio, fine sand is fashioned and solidified into a multitude of decorative and useful objects.

ATELIER YSO
(by appointment)
Tel: (418) 986-2222
ysoflash@hotmail.com
The young glass blower Ysoline Vallée produces decorative objects, including the Coupes Folles (Wild Cups) collection featuring a myriad

of shapes and colors, as well as twisted, etched, and thermoshaped bottles.

LAURENTIANS

ATELIER BERNARD CHAUDRON
2449, chemin de l'Île
Val-David, PQ
Canada J0T 2N0
Tel: (819) 322-3944
Fax: (819) 322-7237
info@chaudron.ca
This master coppersmith creates unique tableware that is both contemporary and traditional. The studio presents pewter pieces that have been hammered and engraved according to traditional techniques.

ALAIN RHÉAUME INC.
130, 2ᵉ Rue
Grandes-Piles, PQ
Canada G0X 1H0

Tel: (819) 538-0428
Fax: (819) 538-2562
American movie stars come here to order top-of-the-line cedar canoes, acclaimed for their fluid beauty and strength. Paddling a six- or nine-foot (two- to three-meter) canoe is an indescribable sensation. The curve of the hull determines whether it is used on a lake or river

GALERIE GAÉTAN-BEAUDIN
2435, rue de l'Église
Val-David, PQ
Canada J0T 2N0
Tel: (819) 322-6868
expo@1001pots.com
Every year since 1989, the studio-gallery has held a large ceramics exhibition in mid-July entitled *1001 Pots*, presenting contemporary and traditional works by Québécois potters.

MONTREAL

INDIANICA
79, rue Saint-Paul Est
Montreal, PQ
Canada H2Y 3R1
Tel: (514) 866-1267
Fax: (514) 866-8988
indianica@bellnet.com
This shop is filled with First Nations handicrafts: rugs, clothing, moccasins, furs and pelts, decorative accessories and objects, and traditional jewelry and sculpture. The shop presents pretty birchbark baskets made by the Atikamek people.

MAISON DE CALICO
324, Bord-du-Lac
Pointe-Claire, PQ
Canada H9S 4L7
Tel: (514) 695-0728
Fax: (514) 695-7479
info@maisondecalico.com
This establishment is a school, gift shop, and

tearoom, where customers can get everything they need to make quilts (supplies, books, patterns, fabric). You can also purchase lovely quilts made by the students.

ST. LAWRENCE PLAIN

COLLECTION NOUVELLE-FRANCE
(by appointment)
Tel: (450) 658-6786
coll.nouvellefrance@videotro.ca
The ceramicist Michel Nicol reproduces eighteenth-century pottery, including work that comes from Saintonge in France. These reproductions are as beautiful as the original pieces discovered during archeological digs; they are available at numerous historical sites in Quebec and at the Pointe-à-Callière museum shop in Montreal.

FRANCE HERVIEUX

(by appointment)
Tel: (450) 589-6309
france.hervieux@sympatico.ca
Fiber creations are a rich heritage in Quebec, and this arrowhead sash maker has no intention of sacrificing traditional techniques to fashion trends. Since 1988, this resident of L'Assomption (in Lanaudière) has been promoting the expertise of local craftsmen.

QUEBEC CITY AND REGION

ÉRIC TARDIF

585, rue de Magellan, apt. 202
Quebec, PQ
Canada G1K 9E8
Tel: (418) 640-3372
info@erictardif.com
The sculptor steams and bends ash, elm, and walnut to create fluid and stream-lined birds. He received first prize from the Janet Sumner Memorial Awards in New York in 2003.

LA MAILLOCHE

58, rue Sous-le-Fort
Quebec, PQ
Canada G1K 4G8
Tel: (418) 694-0445
Fax: (418) 694-1571
mailloch@globetrotter.net
Glass-blower Jean Vallières has won several international awards; he produces one-of-a-kind decorative and utilitarian objects. His studio is a small museum and shop, as well as an ecomuseum

where visitors can learn about glass production techniques.

PAPETERIE SAINT-GILLES

304, rue Félix-Antoine-Savard, C.P. 40
Les Éboulements
Saint-Joseph-de-la-Rive, PQ
Canada G0A 3Y0
Tel: (418) 635-2430
Fax: (418) 635-2613
papier@papeteriesaintgilles.com
Visit the Papeterie Saint-Gilles to learn about traditional paper-making techniques. The Saint-Gilles mottled paper changes with the seasons. The trademark flowers and plants that are incorporated into the sheets of paper are picked by hand and frozen, so that they retain all their color.

SAGUENAY-LAC-SAINT-JEAN

The Saguenay-Lac-Saint-Jean region is well known for its catalognes. It is also a major quilt-producing area, notably in the village of Sainte-Rose-du-Nord. Contact the Cercle des Fermières for individual towns via the regional tourist office.

YVONNE BÉLANGER

(by appointment)
Tel: (418) 674-2610
The beauty and exquisite warmth of the *catalogne* fully justify the long hours of work required to create one. This Saint-Fulgence weaver pays special attention to the texture and colors to create unique and personal works.

CAFÉS

CÔTE NORD

CAFÉ BOHÊME

239, rue des Pionniers
Tadoussac, PQ
Canada G0T 2A0
Tel: (418) 235-1180
Fax: (418) 235-1335
The café-restaurant organizes lively literary evening events. Open from Easter to October.

LAURENTIANS

LA PIERRE ANGULAIRE

39, chemin des Loisirs
Saint-Élie-de-Caxton, PQ
Canada G0X 2N0
Tel: (819) 268-3393
Fax: (819) 268-2293
info@pierre-angulaire.qc.ca
The house, with weathered wood siding surrounded by flowers, houses a unique café. The house is built against a stone face; indeed, one of the walls is formed by an immense rock.

QUEBEC CITY (AND REGION)

KRIEGHOFF

1089, avenue Cartier
Quebec, PQ
Canada G1R 2S6
Tel: (418) 522-3711
Fax: (418) 647-1429
info@cafekrieghoff.qc.ca
The welcoming atmosphere in this establishment will make you want to linger over a good coffee and perhaps a newspaper. You can also enjoy a light snack and deep conservations with friends.

FOOD

APPALACHIANS

(Eastern Townships-Gaspé Peninsula)

ABBAYE SAINT-BENOÎT

(cheese)
Saint-Benoît-du-Lac, PQ
Canada J0B 2M0
Tel: (819) 843-4336
Fax: (819) 843-3199
fromagerie@st-benoit-du-lac.com
The enchanting location looks like somewhere in the Alps. The Saint-Benoît abbey on Lake Memphremagog produces fourteen different types of excellent cheese, including a semi-soft Bleu Bénédictin, a blue cheese, creamy in the center, which evokes flavors of mushrooms and lightly salted rich cream.

ATKINS & FRÈRES ENR.

1, Chanoine-Richard
Mont-Louis, Gaspésie, PQ
Canada G0E 1T0
Tel. and Fax:
(418) 797-5059
atkinsjh@globetrotter.net
This small company special-izes in smoked fish and seafood from the Gaspé Peninsula. It uses a horizon-tal smoking process so that the smoke flows more rapidly over the surface. This tech-nique enhances the subtle, delicate, natural flavor of salmon, mussels, shrimp, and scallops. The smoke-house has also innovated with its smoked squid confit.

BLANCS CÔTEAUX

(vineyard)
1046, route 202
Dunham, PQ
Canada J0E 1M0
Tel: (450) 295-3503
govino@acbm.qc.ca
This is a charming small vineyard with a lovely shop. You can purchase a delicious cider ice cream and some interesting wines such as the Vendange de Bacchus, a fruity dry white wine with a hint of apricot and peach.

ENTREPRISES DE LA FERME CHIMO (cheese)

1705, bd Douglas
Douglastown, Gaspé, PQ
Canada G4X 2W9
Tel: (418) 368-4102
Fax: (418) 368-0071
fchimo@globetrotter.net
The small cheese-maker stands out for the quality of its products: only milk from their own goats goes into the production of their five cheeses, which are served at the Gîte du Mont-Albert. In the summer, guided tours end with a tasting of their products, including the pop-ular Corsaire, a ripened Camembert-type cheese with a slight hazelnut flavor.

L'ORPAILLEUR

1086, route 202
C.P. 339
Dunham, PQ
Canada J0E 1M0
Tel: (450) 295-2763
Fax: (450) 295-3112

info@orpailleur.ca

The wines produced by the large Québécois vineyard never cease to amaze, particularly La Marquise, a fortified wine infused with fruit. This wine has received international awards.

LOWER ST. LAWRENCE

BOULANGERIE NIEMAND

82, avenue Morel
Kamouraska, PQ
Canada G0L 1M0
Tel: (418) 492-1236
The Victorian residence is now a bakery producing organic bread from stone-ground flour made here. It is open from mid-April to late October.

BREUGHEL MICROBREWERY

68, route 132
Saint-Germain-de-Kamouraska, PQ
Canada G0L 3G0
Tel: (418) 492-3693
breughel@mac.com
The old farmhouse furnished with antiques is actually a microbrewery where visitors can taste a local specialty, the Kamour. It's light beer with Belgian yeast, fermented a second time once bottled; it contains no chemical products.

MAISON DE LA PRUNE

129, route 132 Est
Saint-André-de-Kamouraska, PQ
Canada G0L 2H0

Tel: (418) 493-2616
Fax: (418) 493-2149
An orchard and restored general store that was built in 1840. The plums, particularly the Damas, are bottled in vinegar with herbs, or transformed into jelly and syrup.

LA SEIGNEURIE DES AULNAIES

525, de la Seigneurie
Saint-Roch-des-Aulnaies, PQ
Canada G0R 4E0
Tel: (418) 354-2800
Fax: (418) 354-2804
lemoulin@globetrotter.net
Constructed in 1850, this manor house illustrates the wealth of the merchant class in the nineteenth century. The mill, built in 1852, still produces the flour that can be purchased in the shop.

ÎLES DE LA MADELEINE

FROMAGERIE DU PIED-DE-VENT

149, chemin de la Pointe-Basse
C.P. 220
Havre-aux-Maisons, PQ
Canada G0B 1K0
Tel. and Fax:
(418) 969-9292
piedvent@duclos.net
The cows meandering peacefully among the dunes, just steps from the sea, paint a charmingly bucolic portrait. This small cheese producer makes raw milk cheese, notably a delicious washed rind, soft-curd cheese, le Pied-de-Vent.

Montreal's three public markets share the same website:
info@marchespublics-mtl.com

MARCHÉ ATWATER

138, avenue Atwater
Montreal, PQ
Canada H4C 2H6
Tel: (514) 937-7754
Situated along the Lachine Canal, the Marché Atwater was constructed in 1933. Under the handsome clock tower are a number of specialized shops, where shoppers can find foie gras, game, and a large selection of Québécois cheeses.

LE FUMOIR D'ANTAN

27, chemin du Quai
R.R. 1
Havre-aux-Maisons, PQ
Canada G0B 1K0
Tel: (418) 969-4907
Fax: (418) 969-4909
micheline.vigneau@sympatico.ca
The Arseneau family has been fishing and producing smoked herring since 1940. This family-run company has maintained its old-fashioned quality. The smokehouse has become an "economuseum", where visitors can learn about traditional fish smoking techniques. It's definitely authentic, with thousands of herrings hanging in the smokehouse.

MARKETS

MARCHÉ JEAN TALON

7075, avenue Casgrain
Montreal, PQ
Canada H2S 3A3
Tel: (514) 277-1588
Fax: (514) 277-1379
This lively and flower-filled market is in the heart of Little Italy. The Marché Jean Talon specializes in fresh vegetables from all over the region. It also has a few surprising shops: the Marché des Saveurs du Québec shop offers spirits, cider, wine, and a diverse selection of delicious regional products. Smoked products from Frères Atkins on the Gaspé Peninsula are also available

here. The many small multiethnic restaurants all around the market add to the fun ambiance.

MARCHÉ MAISONNEUVE

4445, rue Ontario Est
Montreal, PQ
Canada H1V 3V3
Tel: (514) 937-7774
Fax: (514) 937-7688
The stands in the Marché Maisonneuve are filled with regional vegetables as well as a large selection of flowers. They also offer an abundance of diverse organic products.

LAURENTIANS

ABBAYE OKA (store)

1500, chemin d'Oka
Oka, PQ
Canada J0N 1E0
Tel: (450) 479-6170
Fax: (450) 479-6861
magasin@abbayeoka.com
Although the famous Oka cheese is no longer completely handmade by the Cistercians, it is still a trademark Quebec product, like cheddar. Created in 1893, the semi-soft strong-flavored cheese is similar to Port Salut, made at the Entrammes monastery in France.

GOURMET SAUVAGE

(by appointment)

Tel: (450) 229-3277
Fax: (450) 229-3312
gourmet.sauvage@qc.aira.com
There are only a dozen or so companies of this type in Quebec. Gourmet Sauvage processes fruit, vegetables, and wild tubers into various products, including jellies, flours, and vinegars. These products are also sold abroad.

INTERMIEL

10291, rang de La Fresnière
Mirabel Saint-Benoît, PQ
Canada J7N 3M3
Tel: (450) 258-2713
Fax: (450) 258-2708
intermiel@sympatico.ca
One of Quebec's largest bee farms, where the specialty is mead (honey wine).

Intermiel also produces maple syrup.

MONTREAL

FAIRMOUNT BAGEL
74, rue Fairmount Ouest
Montreal, PQ
Canada H2T 2M2
Tel: (514) 272-0667
Fax: (514) 272-0604
Montreal's first baker to offer bagels opened in 1949 on Rue Fairmount. Day and night, you can enjoy these delicious baked goods cooked in a wood-burning oven.

R.J. BREWERY
5585, rue de la Roche
Montreal, PQ
Canada H2J 3K3
Tel: (514) 274-4941
Fax: (514) 274-6138
visite@brasseursrj.com
Locally produced beer started to become popular in Quebec more than a decade ago. The R.J. brewery includes three Québécois microbreweries. One of them, Le Cheval Blanc, makes seasonal beers along with its ales: the Tord-vis in the spring, a beer with undertones of smoky malt and maple syrup; the Sainte-Paix flavored with cherries and apples in the summer; and finally, the Snoreau, a winter beer with spices, barley, and cranberries.

L'AMÈRE À BOIRE
2049, rue Saint-Denis
Montreal, PQ
Canada H2X 3K8
Tel: (514) 282-7448
Fax: (514) 282-5453
info@amereaboire.com
A small brewery and restaurant in the heart of Montreal's Latin Quarter. The brewery offers unpasteurized, unfiltered beer, and a menu featuring crème brûlée made with stout.

MONTREAL POOL ROOM
1200, bd Saint-Laurent
Montreal, PQ
Canada H2X 2S5
Tel: (514) 396-0460
In the heart of one of Montreal's seedier neighborhoods, this temple to the hot dog is one of the city's institutions, with food available day and night. People order one, two, and even three *steamé* (so-called because the bun that coutains the hot dog is steamed).

SCHWARTZ'S
3895, bd Saint-Laurent
Montreal, PQ
Canada H2W 1X9
Tel: (514) 842-4813
This Montreal deli has been making smoked meat sandwiches since 1930. The inimitable flavor can be found all around the world, even in Tokyo.

ST. LAWRENCE PLAIN

CENTRE D'INTERPRÉTATION DE LA CANNEBERGE
80, rue Principale
C.P. 140
Saint-Louis-de-Blandford, PQ
Canada G0Z 1B0
Tel: (819) 364-5112
Fax: (819) 364-2781
cic@boisfrancs.qc.ca
Every year during harvest season, a large tent is set up in late October next to the cranberry bogs of a large producer where visitors can learn all about cranberries.

CLOS SAINT-DENIS
1149, chemin des Patriotes (route 133)
Saint-Denis-sur-Richelieu, PQ
Canada J0H 1K0
Tel: (450) 787-3766
Fax: (450) 787-9956
info@clos-saint-denis.qc.ca
Clos Saint-Denis, a vineyard and orchard, is well known for its Pomme de Glace, which is perfect served with foie gras.

FROMAGERIE ÉCO-DÉLICES
766, rang 9 Est
Plessisville, PQ
Canada G6L 2Y2
Tel: (819) 362-7472
Fax: (819) 362-1344
ecodelic@ivic.qc.ca
In 1996, this family-run establishment, already a certified organic farm, obtained an authorization to produce the famous French Mamirolle cheese in Canada. Its Mamirolle reproduces the delicious flavor of the original, and is even softer and creamier. Another semi-soft cheese, the Délice des Appalaches, has a slight apple flavor, as it is ripened in Pomme de Glace, the famous cider produced by the Clos Saint-Denis apple orchards.

UNIBROUE
80, rue des Carrières
Chambly, PQ
Canada J3L 2H6
Tel: (450) 658-7658
Fax: (450) 658-9195
info@unibroue.com
A major producer of internationally famous though locally made beers, brewed according to age-old techniques.

VERGERS LAFRANCE
1473, chemin Principal
Saint-Joseph-du-Lac, PQ
Canada J0N 1M0
Tel: (450) 491-7859
Fax: (450) 491-7528
info@lesvergerslafrance.com
This producer makes cider by blending several types of perfectly ripe apples (seventeen in all, including the Macintosh, the Lobo, and the Cortland). Popular products include the Pomme de Neige, an ice cider that has received several awards, and the Cuvée Lafrance, a delicate sparkling cider.

QUEBEC CITY AND REGION

LA BARBERIE
310, rue Saint-Roch
Quebec, PQ
Canada G1K 6S2
Tel: (418) 522-4373
Fax: (418) 522-5283
information@labarberie.com
The microbrewery is a cooperative of professional brewers based in the Saint-Roch neighborhood. The ale is brewed in small quantities, according to traditional methods.

LUC MAILLOUX
(cheese)
150, rue Angélique
Saint-Basile-de-Portneuf, PQ
Canada G0A 3G0
Tel. and Fax:
(418) 329-3080
lucmailloux@globetrotter.net
lesfromagesstbasile@hotmail.com
The first raw-milk Québécois cheese, La Sainte-Basile was produced at the experimental farm Piluma. Ever since, its cheeses have been ranked consistently among the best. These include the famous raw-milk Lechevalier Mailloux.

J.A. MOISAN
(grocery store)
699, rue Saint-Jean
Quebec, PQ
Canada G1R 1P7
Tel: (418) 522-0685
info@jamoisan.com
The oldest grocery store in North America offers a selection of fine regional products in a typical old-style setting.

LAITERIE CHARLEVOIX INC.
1167, bd Mgr-de-Laval
Baie-Saint-Paul, PQ
Canada G3Z 2W7
Tel: (418) 435-2184
Fax: (418) 435-6976
labbe@charlevoix.net
Member of the Route des

Saveurs de Charlevoix and a cheese "economuseum," this dairy produces delicious cheeses, including the fresh (and eight-year-old) cheddar, Charlevoix and the Fleurmier, a soft cheese with a delicate flavor of almonds. In the morning, visitors can watch the various stages of cheese production. It is also possible to taste the cheese and other regional specialties.

LA MAISON D'AFFINAGE MAURICE DUFOUR
1339, bd Mgr-de-Laval
Baie-Saint-Paul, PQ
Canada G3Z 2X6
Tel: (418) 435-5692
Fax: (418) 435-6334
Discover the production methods used to make the famous local cheese, the Migneron de Charlevoix and Ciel de Charlevoix. Visitors can taste the cheeses, served with other regional products.

SAGUENAY-LAC-SAINT-JEAN

NOTRE-DAME DE MISTASSINI MONASTERY
100, route des Trappistes
Dolbeau-Mistassini, PQ
Canada G8L 5E5
Tel: (418) 276-0491
Fax: (418) 276-8885
Situated north of Lac Saint-Jean, this monastery offers a number of products, including delicious, fresh blueberries dipped in chocolate—to be eaten on the spot, before they lose their flavor.

ACCOMMODATION

APPALACHIANS
(Eastern Townships-Gaspé Peninsula)

AUBERGE CHÂTEAU DU LAC
85, rue Merry Sud
Magog, PQ
Canada J1X 3L2
Tel: (819) 868-1666
Fax: (819) 868-9989
info@aubergedulac.com
This inn offers Anglo-Saxon distinction with the refinement of classic French cuisine in a very typical Eastern Townships settings. Specialties include a delicious rack of lamb. The inn also has a large number of Impressionist-style paintings by the owner, who signs her works Christine Carrière. In addition to enjoying the artwork, guests can explore the region by bike, right from the inn.

AUBERGE HATLEY
325, chemin Virgin
North Hatley, PQ
Canada J0B 2C0
Tel: (819) 842-2451
Fax: (819) 842-2907
auberge.hatley@northhatley.com
Flowers, a fountain, and goldfish greet guests at the entrance, setting the tone for a stay that is generally organized around the pleasures of the fine restaurant. Don't miss a visit to the wine cellar.

BLEU-SUR-MER
504, route 132

Port-Daniel-Gascons, PQ
Canada G0C 2N0
Tel: (418) 396-2573
info@bleusurmer.com
This relaxing inn is the only place on the Gaspé Peninsula where the interior and exterior spaces have been designed according to the principles of feng shui. The landscaping, choice of colors, and natural materials create a harmonious and intimate effect. Top-notch food is served at breakfast, where guests can enjoy a tempting selection of fresh local products.

GÎTE DU MONT-ALBERT
2001, route du Parc
Sainte-Anne-des-Monts, PQ
Canada G4V 2E4
Tel: (418) 763-2288
Fax: (418) 763-7803
gitmtalb@sepaq.com
Sports lovers flock to this popular mountain destination, located within a park that boasts some of the highest mountains in Quebec. The Gîte du Mont-Albert is acclaimed for its comfortable and independent cabins; it still has the retro charm of the 1930s and 1950s. The service is great, and the Gaspé cuisine features fresh fish and seafood, along with traditional dishes.

MANOIR HOVEY
575, chemin Hovey
North Hatley, PQ
Canada J0B 2C0
Tel: (819) 842-2421
Fax: (819) 842-2248
manhovey@manoirhovey.com

This is a romantic place to stay, with luxurious rooms and individually decorated suites. One of them, the Bouleaux, combines modern design with backwoods charm.

PASSE-PARTOUT
167, bd Pierre-Laporte
Cowansville, PQ
Canada J2K 2G3
Tel: (450) 260-1678
info@passepartout.ca
This pretty nineteenth-century farmhouse was converted into a friendly bed-and-breakfast, set amid a lush bucolic setting. The décor inside reflects the landscape outside. Each of the four upstairs bedrooms is decorated differently, including one with an Asian theme.

LOWER ST. LAWRENCE

AUBERGE DU MANGE GRENOUILLE
148, rue Sainte-Cécile
Le Bic, PQ
Canada G0L 1B0
Tel: (418) 736-5656
Fax: (418) 736-5657
Don't miss the Mange Grenouille, situated near the Parc du Bic. Guests come from all over Quebec to enjoy the fine cuisine, which features regional products, including lamb and duck. Open from early May to mid-October.

AU REFUGE DU VIEUX LOUP DE MER
C.P. 88
Rimouski, PQ

Canada G5L 7B7
Tel: (418) 750-5915
martin.gagnon@cgocable.ca
Martin Gagnon proposes four picturesque cabins for his guests, all furnished with antiques and recycled objects. Perched on the cliff of Baie Rose, one of these cabins, the Loup-Marin, has a spectacular view of the Bic islands.

CÔTE NORD

HÔTEL TADOUSSAC
165, rue Bord-de-l'Eau
Tadoussac, PQ
Canada G0T 2A0
Tel: (418) 235-4421
Fax: (418) 235-4607
receptiontad@groupedufour.com
Guests may recognize the Hotel New Hampshire from the film of the same name inspired by John Irving's novel. Indeed, some of the outside scenes were filmed at the Hôtel Tadoussac. It's not surprising, as this elegant hotel was constructed on a magnificent site. The hotel closes from mid-October to mid-May.

ÎLES DE LA MADELEINE

AU SALANGE
C.P. 1230
Cap-aux-Meules, PQ
Canada G0B 1B0
Tel: (418) 969-4322
Fax: (418) 969-4321
ausalange@duclos.net
This wooden house with large windows is a top-notch

bed-and-breakfast. Located one hundred feet (thirty meters) from the sea at the edge of a bay, Au Salange offers a friendly, contemporary setting. The scents and flavors of the island appear at the breakfast table with, among other dishes, scrambled eggs with smoked herring or a terrine of sea wolf.

CHEZ MCLEAN
Île-d'Entrée, PQ
Canada G0B 1C0
Tel: (418) 986-4541
The old-fashioned charm of this former lighthouse-keeper's house is highly popular among guests, who can bring in food and cook their own meals. This is the only place to stay on Entry Island, so it's a good idea to reserve ahead. The bed-and-breakfast is closed from October to late March.

LAURENTIANS

AUBERGE LE BALUCHON
3550, chemin des Trembles
Saint-Paulin, PQ
Canada J0K 3G0
Tel: (819) 268-2555
Fax: (819) 268-5234
info@baluchon.com
Le Baluchon has a reputation for excellence, for the beauty of the site as well as the fine cuisine and the spa. The summer theater is also innovative: the play is staged on the river, with the actors and spectators in *rabaskas** (long canoes).

CÔTÉ NORD (vacation center)
141, Tour-du-Lac
Lac-Supérieur, PQ
Canada J0T 1P0
Tel: (819) 688-5201
info@cotenord.ca
This hybrid concept is an unusual real-estate development consisting of sixty superbly outfitted log cabins and a charming inn, situated in the heart of the Laurentian forest. The establishment also offers guests the possibilities of staying in one of four extremely comfortable "rustic" log cabins.

HÔTEL SACACOMIE
4000, rang Sacacomie
Saint-Alexis-des-Monts, PQ
Canada J0K 1V0
Tel: (819) 265-4444
Fax: (819) 265-4445
info@sacacomie.com
Summer and winter, the experience starts the moment you step into a float plane in Montreal or Quebec City (reservations available from the hotel), and continues as the plane lands amid wild flowers and herbs.

MONTREAL

HÔTEL GAULT
449, rue Sainte-Hélène
Montreal, PQ
Canada H2Y 2K9
Tel: (514) 904-1616
Fax: (514) 904-1717
info@hotelgault.com
The décor on the ground floor alternates between concrete and steel. The treatment of these materials

suggests the passage from the past to the present day. Everything is clear and airy. In addition, the smiling, friendly staff warms up the spare interiors.

HÔTEL TERRASSE ROYALE
5225, Côte-des-Neiges
Montreal, PQ
Canada H3T 1Y1
Tel: (514) 739-6391
Fax: (514) 342-2512
sejour@terrasse-royale.com
Comfortable apartments with an indoor garage, situated a few minutes from downtown and near the Parc du Mont-Royal.

HÔTEL SAINT-PAUL
355, rue McGill
Montreal, PQ
Canada H2Y 2E8
Tel: (514) 380-2222
Fax: (514) 380-2200
info@hotelstpaul.com
The Hôtel Saint-Paul is a series of sophisticated spaces that combine fluid textures and sensual materials with strictly minimalist forms. The establishment draws a diverse clientele, but is specially known for its young, trendy guests who love the elegant, pure lines.

ST. LAWRENCE PLAIN

SUCRERIE DE LA MONTAGNE
300, rang Saint-Georges
Rigaud, PQ
Canada J0P 1P0
Tel: (450) 451-0831

Fax: (450) 451-0340
info@sucreriedelamontagne.com
The *sucrerie* is intended to preserve the character of the traditional sugarhouse, a symbol of Québécois hospitality and tradition. The general store is also a good place to pick up a few items, including butter, sugar, and maple jelly, all made here. The store also stocks *catalognes* and other traditional works.

QUEBEC CITY AND REGION

AU PETIT HÔTEL
3, rue des Ursulines
Québec, PQ
Canada G1R 3Y6
Tel: (418) 694-0965
aupetithotel@sympatico.ca
This charming Victorian building, constructed in 1898, is situated on a quiet small street. It once belonged to the architect Charles Baillargé, who drew up his plans in this house. The sixteen-room bed-and-breakfast still has its original plaster ceiling moldings, fireplace, and elaborate staircase. This is a great inn valued for its friendly service, proximity to the main sites in Old Quebec, shops, and good restaurants.

AU VIEUX FOYER
2687, chemin Royal
Saint-Pierre-de-l'Île-d'Orléans, PQ
Canada G0A 4E0
Tel: (418) 828-9171
info@auvieuxfoyer.qc.ca

Lush greenery surrounds this establishment, which was built in the early nineteenth century. The architecture evokes times past; the furnishings and antique objects all contribute to the charm of this bed-and-breakfast.

AUBERGE SAINT-ANTOINE
8, rue Saint-Antoine
Quebec, PQ
Canada G1K 4C9
Tel: (418) 692-2211
Fax: (418) 692-1177
info@martincarpentier.com
Named one of the best getaways by the Condé Nast Traveler Gold List. This charming hotel is situated in a building that was constructed in the eighteenth century in the Old Port of Quebec City. It offers a romantic stay, filled with history, as each of the thirty rooms has its own unique character. An archeological dig, undertaken in conjunction with a remodeling project, unearthed 5,000 artifacts, 250 of which are now on permanent display at the hotel.

CHÂTEAU FRONTENAC
1, rue des Carrières
Quebec, PQ
Canada G1R 4P5
Tel: (418) 692-3861
Fax: (418) 692-1751
chateaufrontenac@fairmont.com
The Château Frontenac is Quebec City's landmark. It overlooks Old Quebec, which has been listed as a UNESCO

World Heritage Site. This hotel sets the standard for quality accommodation and restaurant fare in the provincial capital. Run by the acclaimed chef Jean Soulard, Le Champlain, the hotel's restaurant offers a new style of Québécois cuisine, combining refinement and regional diversity.

DOMINION 1912
126, rue Saint-Pierre
Quebec, PQ
Canada G1K 4A8
Tel: (418) 692-2224
Fax: (418) 692-4403
reservations@hoteldominion.com
This boutique hotel was created in the first skyscraper built in Quebec City in 1912.

Designer and architect Viateur Michaud has successfully combined modernism and classicism in his décor. The rooms were designed in his office, even before the hotel itself was created; they can be remodeled whenever needed to satisfy the highest standards of comfort of this lovely establishment.

HÔTEL DE GLACE
143, route Duchesnay,
Pavillon l'Aigle
Sainte-Catherine-de-la-Jacques-Cartier, PQ
Canada G0A 3M0
Tel: (418) 875-4522
Fax: (418) 875-2833
information@icehotel-canada.com
For some people, the hardest part is relaxing in a Jacuzzi, placed in a bedroom constructed of snow and ice. For others, it's strange to spend the night dancing in the ice club, under the multicolored spotlights.

MANOIR RICHELIEU
181, rue Richelieu
La Malbaie, PQ
Canada G5A 1X7
Tel: (418) 665-3703
Fax: (418) 665-8131
manoirrichelieu@fairmont.com
The various interiors at the Manoir Richelieu illustrate another era. Today, guests come to the hotel for its comfort, landscapes, casino, and fine dining. The hotel is along the Charlevoix Route des Saveurs.

SAGUENAY-LAC-SAINT-JEAN

AVENTURE MIKUAN II
1562, rue Ouiatchouan
Mashteuiatsh, PQ
Canada G0W 2H0
Tel: (418) 275-2949
Fax: (418) 275-6691
The Ashuapmushuan ("where you observe the origins" in the Innu language) wildlife reserve was a favorite place for the Innu who hunted animals for the fur trade. The establishment, in the midst of the untamed wilds, teaches guests about ancestral ways of life, including how to find medicinal plants.

CAP AU LESTE POURVOIRIE
551, chemin Cap-au-Leste
Sainte-Rose-du-Nord, PQ
Canada G0V 1T0
Tel: (418) 675-2000/1271
Fax: (418) 675-1232
contact@capauleste.com
The view over the Saguenay marine park is spectacular, and the setting is serene, both for outdoor enthusiasts and guests on working vacations. The rustic décor of the Cap au Leste is perfect for theme events which sometimes take place in the winter, such as oldtimer story telling.

MUSEUMS AND INTERPRETATION CENTERS

APPALACHIANS
(Eastern Townships-Gaspé Peninsula)

MAGASIN GÉNÉRAL HISTORIQUE
32, rue Bonfils
Anse-à-Beaufils
Percé, PQ
Canada G0C 1G0
Tel: (418) 782-2225
Fax: (418) 782-5475
This authentic general store from the 1930s has been entirely restored, although the woodwork is original; it contains many common objects from the period. The shopkeepers in period costumes play out scenes of everyday life, much to the pleasure of visitors.

MUSÉE ACADIEN DU QUÉBEC
95, avenue Port-Royal
Bonaventure, PQ
Canada G0C 1E0
Tel: (418) 534-4000
Fax: (418) 534-4105
reception@museeacadien.com
A historical and ethnological museum that recounts the life and settlements in Quebec of the Acadians from the province of New Brunswick.

MUSÉE LE CHAFAUD
145, route 132 Ouest
Anse-à-Beaufils
Percé, PQ
Canada G0C 2L0
Tel: (418) 782-5100
Fax: (418) 782-5565
lebjl@globetrotter.net
A multidisciplinary museum that was created in an old building that belonged to the omnipresent Charles Robin company and was used to process and dry cod. Constructed in 1845, the building now hosts large national and international visual arts exhibitions and is an interpretation center for the history of the surrounding area.

LA VIEILLE USINE DE L'ANSE-À-BEAUFILS
55, rue Bonfils
Anse-à-Beaufils
Percé, PQ
Canada G0C 1G0
Tel: (418) 782-2277
Fax: (418) 782-5800
lavieilleusine@globetrotter.net
The abandoned factory was used as a fish processing plant in 1928 and was recently-transformed into a tourist and cultural venue. The space has a theater, an interpretation center, and an exhibition center where more than forty regional artists exhibit their contemporary work alongside traditional folk art.

CÔTE NORD

MAISON CHAUVIN
157, rue Bord-de-l'Eau
Tadoussac, PQ
Canada G0T 2A0
Tel: (418) 235-4657
This establishment was the first fur trading post, and celebrated its 400th year in 2000. This was also the first attempt to create a permanent settlement in Quebec.

ÎLES DE LA MADELEINE

MUSÉE DE LA MER
1023, route 199, Pointe Shea
C.P. 69
Havre-Aubert, PQ
Canada G0B 1J0
Tel: (418) 937-5711
Fax: (418) 937-2449
This ethnological museum recounts the history of the Îles de la Madeleine.

LAURENTIAN MOUNTAINS

MANOIR PAPINEAU
500, rue Notre-Dame
Montebello, PQ
Canada J0V 1L0
Tel: (819) 423-6965
Fax: (819) 423-6455
parcscanada-que@pc.gc.ca
Situated on the banks of the Ottawa River, this historic site presents the admirable restoration of the vacation home of Louis-Joseph Papineau, a major figure in Canadian history. It is a lovely example of a nineteenth-century seigneurial manor in Quebec. The rear balcony of this imposing residence has decorative elements that have been fully catalogued and studied.

MUSÉE D'ART DE JOLIETTE
145, rue Wilfrid-Corbeil
Joliette, PQ
Canada J6E 4T4
Tel: (450) 756-0311
Fax: (450) 756-6511
musee.joliette@citenet.net
This museum presents a surprising collection of religious artwork, including canvases and sacred objects. The museum's program also includes many workshops and exhibitions, with, for example, a show of the representation of arrowhead sashes in Canadian art and another presenting contemporary works in steel and concrete by the Quebec artist Claude Mongrain.

MONTREAL

MUSÉE D'ART CONTEMPORAIN DE MONTRÉAL
185, rue Sainte-Catherine Ouest
Montreal, PQ
Canada H2X 3X5
Tel: (514) 847-6226
Fax: (514) 847-6291
This museum hosts shows of contemporary Québécois, Canadian, and international artwork. It also presents multimedia work, notably performances of new dance, experimental theater, and contemporary music.

MUSÉE DES BEAUX-ARTS DE MONTRÉAL
Pavillons Hornstein et Stewart
1379, rue Sherbrooke Ouest
Pavillon Desmarais
1380, rue Sherbrooke Ouest
C.P. 3000, Succ. H
Montreal, PQ
Canada H3G 2T9
Tel: (514) 285-2000
A venue for international traveling exhibitions. The museum also houses a collection of decorative and contemporary art, as well as work from ancient cultures.

MUSÉE MCCORD
690, rue Sherbrooke Ouest
Montreal, PQ
Canada H3A 1E9
Tel: (514) 398-7100
Fax: (514) 398-5045
info@mccord.mcgill.ca
This museum is devoted to the preservation of Canadian history and historical research. It has a large collection of ethnological, archaeological, and decorative objects.

MUSÉE POINTE-À-CALLIÈRE
350, place Royale
Montreal, PQ
Canada H2Y 3Y5
Tel: (514) 872-9150
Fax: (514) 872-9151
info@pacmusee.qc.ca
The archeology and history of Montreal, from its First Nations origins to the present, can be discovered in this audaciously contemporary building opposite the Old Port.

ST. LAWRENCE PLAIN

FORGES-DU-SAINT-MAURICE
10000, bd. des Forges
Trois-Rivières, PQ
Canada G9C 1B1
Tel: (819) 378-5116
Fax: (819) 378-0887
parcscanada-que@pc.gc.ca
This was Canada's first ironworks, created in 1733 on the Saint-Maurice River at Trois-Rivières, under French rule. The Forges were used to produce iron objects, primarily for the shipbuilding industry. The visit to this archeological site, including the forge and the blast furnace, shows how the industry has changed over the centuries. The site also has a sound and light show.

ÎLE-DES-MOULINS
867, rue Saint-Pierre
Terrebonne, PQ
Canada J6W 1E6
Tel: (450) 471-0619
Fax: (450) 471-8311
iledesmoulins@qc.aira.com
This pre-industrial nineteenth-century village includes several mills, a seigniorial office, a baker, and a charming local home dating to 1760. It hosts many cultural events, including the Fête des Voyageurs, which brings to life the adventures of the *voyageurs* of the Northwest Company, a company that made its fortune in the fur trade. The nearby Maison de Pays shop sells local and regional specialties as well as objects made by craftsmen. This is one of the rare places where you can find "authentic" quilts, *catalognes*, and arrowhead sashes by France Hervieux.

INSTITUT QUÉBÉCOIS DE L'ÉRABLE ET MUSÉE DE L'ÉRABLE INC.
1280, rue Trudelle
Plessisville, PQ
Canada G6L 3K4
Tel: (819) 362-9292
Fax: (819) 362-8155
bureau@erable.org
This institute promotes the maple trade, with a history of maple tree growing, sap tapping, and the transformation of sap into numerous products, many of which are available at the institute shop.

QUEBEC CITY AND REGION

MANOIR MAUVIDE-GENEST FONDATION DES SEIGNEURIES DE L'ÎLE D'ORLÉANS
Fondation des Seigneuries de l'Île d'Orléans
1451, chemin Royal
Saint-Jean-de-l'Île-d'Orléans, PQ
Canada G0A 3W0
Tel: (418) 829-2630
Fax: (418) 829-0734
mauvide-genest@oricom.ca
The surgeon Jean Mauvide liked to travel into the village in his gold and burgundy carriage. This may be an anecdotal detail, but it reveals the sophisticated lifestyle of the young colony in the eighteenth century. Visitors will also discover popular beliefs of the time, such as fear of werewolves—illustrated by the cleared forestland around this carefully restored aristocratic residence.

MUSÉE DE CHARLEVOIX
10, chemin du Havre
La Malbaie, PQ

Canada G5A 2Y8
Tel: (418) 665-4411
Fax: (418) 665-4560
info@museedecharlevoix.qc.
ca
The Charlevoix museum is devoted to regional culture and heritage, and is one of the few museums to have a large collection of folk art.

MUSÉE DE LA CIVILISATION

85, rue Dalhousie
C.P. 155, Succ. B
Quebec, PQ
Canada G1K 7A6
Tel: (418) 643-2158
Fax: (418) 646-9705
mcq@mcq.org
The Museum of Civilization is one of the three largest museums in Quebec. It contains the largest ethnographic and historic collection in Quebec, notably many furniture and textile pieces. This museum is also famous for the thematic approach to the exhibitions that it presents.

MUSÉE NATIONAL DES BEAUX-ARTS DU QUÉBEC

1, avenue Wolfe-Montcalm
Quebec, PQ
Canada G1R 5H3
Tel: (418) 643-2150
Fax: (418) 643-5851
info@mnba.qc.ca
The mission of this fine-arts museums to create a living memory of Québécois art. It curates exhibitions from its large collection of works by Québécois artists and hosts international exhibitions.

ONHOÜA CHETEK8E

575, rue Stanislas-Koska
Wendake, PQ
Canada G0A 4V0
Tel: (418) 842-4308
Fax: (418) 842- 3473
wendat@huron-wendat.qc.ca
Located at Wendake, not far from Quebec City, this reconstructed Huron village is a testimony to the vitality and past of this community. Some ceremonies, such as the welcome dance, are still performed. Visitors can sample traditional dishes, such as the beans, game and *sagamité**, served on lovely plates.

SAGUENAY-LAC-SAINT-JEAN

COMPLEXE TOURISTIQUE MARIA-CHAPDELAINE MUSÉE LOUIS-HÉMON

700, route Maria-Chapdelaine
Péribonka, PQ
Canada G0W 2G0
Tel: (418) 374-2177
Fax: (418) 374-2516
museelh@destination.ca
Situated north of Lac Saint-Jean, the Samuel-Bédard house has been classified a historical monument. This is where the French author Louis Hémon wrote his famous novel *Maria Chapdelaine* in 1912.

RESTAURANTS

APPALACHIANS

(Eastern Townships-Gaspé Peninsula)

CAPITAINE HOMARD

180, route de la Mer
C.P. 61
Sainte-Flavie, PQ
Canada G0J 2L0
Tel: (418) 775-8046
capitainehomard@cgocable.
ca
This restaurant on the banks of the St. Lawrence is certainly picturesque. As for the food, it is quite simply delicious.

MAISON DU PÊCHEUR

155, place du Quai
Percé, PQ
Canada G0C 2L0
Tel: (418) 782-5331/ 5326
Fax: (418) 782-5624
pecheur@globetrotter.qc.ca
A restaurant whose fame extends far beyond the borders of the Gaspé Peninsula. The restaurant offers creative interpretations of fish and seafood dishes, as well as other specialties, such as seaweed soup. Cod tongue, a regional specialty, is also on the menu.

LOWER ST. LAWRENCE

MAISON RONDE

183, rang du Mississippi
Saint-Germain-de-Kamouraska, PQ
Canada G0L 3G0

Tel: (418) 492-3036
The Maison Ronde offers a hearty banquet primarily created from its own home-grown products, including Muscovy duck.

ÎLES DE LA MADELEINE

TABLE DES ROY

1188, chemin Lavernière
C.P. 240
Cap-aux-Meules, PQ
Canada G0B 1E0
Tel: (418) 986-3004
Fax: (418) 986-3068
jvigneau@duclos.net
This acclaimed restaurant proposes refined seasonal cuisine made from regional and local products. It is open from June to late September.

LAURENTIANS

BISTRO À CHAMPLAIN

75, chemin Masson
Sainte-Marguerite-du-Lac-Masson, PQ
Canada J0T 1L0
Tel: (450) 228-4988/4949
Fax: (450) 228-4893
info@bistroachamplain.qc.ca
Opened in a general store dating to 1874, this bistro has one of the best wine cellars in North America. The setting combines the rustic look of wood with sophisticated tableware.

L'EAU À LA BOUCHE

3003, bd Sainte-Adèle
(route 117)

Sainte-Adèle, PQ
Canada J8B 2N6
Tel: (450) 229-2991
Fax: (450) 229-7573
eaubouche@sympatico.ca
A member of the Relais et Châteaux chain, L'Eau à la Bouche is both a hotel and famous restaurant, run by the talented chef and owner Anne Desjardins.

MONTREAL

CAFÉ MÉLIÈS

3540, bd Saint-Laurent
Montreal, PQ
Canada H2X 2V1
Tel: (514) 847-9218
Fax: (514) 847-9584
info@cafemelies.com
A visit to the Ex-Centris cinema often spills over into this trendy restaurant, also located in the Ex-Centris complex. The Café Méliès has a clientele of professionals, including many creators working in multimedia; they often meet up in the restaurant lounge to discuss their various projects or simply spend time networking.

CARTET

106, rue McGill
Montreal, PQ
Canada H2Y 2E5
Tel: (514) 871-8887
The food shop offers take-out dishes, as well as simple lunch specialties. Christopher Nouaille also sells the famous lemon tart created by his grandmother,

who opened the Cartet in Paris.

CHEZ L'ÉPICIER
311, rue Saint-Paul Est
Montreal, PQ
Canada H2Y 1H3
Tel: (514) 878-2232
Fax: (514) 878-2239
laurent.godbout@chezlepicier.com
The chef and owner of Chez l'Épicier creates original food that blends contemporary with traditional Québécois cuisine, in the shop near the Marché Bonsecours in Old Montreal.

PIERRE-DU-CALVET
405, rue Bonsecours
Montreal, PQ
Canada H2Y 3C3
Tel: (514) 282-1725
Fax: (514) 282-0456
calvet@pierreducalvet.ca
The historic home of a rich French merchant, Pierre du Calvet, who moved to Montreal in the eighteenth century. Constructed in 1725, the inn houses Les Filles du Roy, a French restaurant that also serves up regional products.

TOQUÉ!
900, place Jean-Paul-Riopelle
Montreal, PQ
Canada H2Z 2B2
Tel: (514) 499-2084
Fax: (514) 499-0292
info@restaurant-toque.com
The chef and owner Normand Laprise was the precursor of the new Québécois cuisine. He creates daring dishes that combine innovative textures and delicious flavors.

ST. LAWRENCE PLAIN

HOSTELLERIE LES TROIS TILLEULS
290, rue Richelieu
Saint-Marc-sur-Richelieu, PQ
Canada J0L 2E0
Tel: (514) 856-7787
Fax: (450) 584-3146
info@lestroistilleuls.com
A member of the Relais et Châteaux chain since 1983, this acclaimed restaurant offers a diverse cuisine based on regional products. Don't miss the black Abitibi sturgeon caviar, wild game, and Québécois cheese.

QUEBEC CITY AND REGION

AUX ANCIENS CANADIENS
34, rue Saint-Louis
C.P. 175
Quebec, PQ
Canada G1R 4P3
Tel: (418) 692-1627
Fax: (418) 692-5419
restaurant@auxanciens-canadiens.qc.ca
Author Philippe Aubert de Gaspé senior wrote his novel *Les Anciens Canadiens* in this house. Today, the residence is devoted to the pleasures of the table. Here guests can enjoy traditional Québécois cuisine in a historic setting.

AUBERGE DES 3 CANARDS
115, côte Bellevue
La Malbaie, PQ
Canada G5A 1Y2
Tel: (418) 665-3761
Fax: (418) 665-4727
info@auberge3canards.com
A friendly luxury inn, which also has an incomparable restaurant.

AUBERGE LA COURTEPOINTE
8, rue Racine
Petite-Rivière-Saint-François, PQ
Canada G0A 2L0
Tel: (418) 632-5858
Fax: (418) 632-5786
lacourtepointe@charlevoix.net
Traditional and refined Québécois cuisine, which showcases products from the Charlevoix region, including the grain-fed Charlevoix veal, and bean soup from beans raised in the inn's own garden.

LE CAFÉ DU CLOCHER PENCHÉ
203, rue Saint-Joseph Est
Quebec, PQ
Canada G1K 3B1
Tel: (418) 640-0597
Fax: (418) 640-0549
clocherpenche@qc.aira.com
This bistro is located in the Saint-Roch neighborhood in a former bank with immense windows. The ambiance is extremely lively and the cuisine is based on regional products, with such specialties as lamb knuckle, blood sausage, and homemade fresh cheese. The restaurant also exhibits work by contemporary figurative Québécois painters.

LE CAFÉ DU MONDE
84, rue Dalhousie
Quebec, PQ
Canada G1K 4B2
Tel: (418) 692-4455
Fax: (418) 692-4448
Paris in Quebec City. This is the trendiest bistro in town, located at Pointe-à-Carcy in the Old Port. French bistro fare with a view of the St. Lawrence River.

CHARLES BAILLARGÉ
57, rue Sainte-Anne
Quebec, PQ
Canada G1R 3X4
Tel: (418) 692-2480
Fax: (418) 692-4652
The Art Deco and château styles of the Hôtel Clarendon extend to the Charles Baillargé, said to be the oldest restaurant in North America. The wood paneling, mirrors, and mahogany tones create a cozy, discreet ambience. The young chef Marc Blouin serves up French-style fare based on regional products, with a subtle blend of flavors and scents, notably cloves and port, or curry and leek. The crème brûlée with maple and raspberry is still one of his great classics.

LE LAURIE RAPHAËL
117, rue Dalhousie
Quebec, PQ
Canada G1K 9C8
Tel: (418) 692-4555
Fax: (418) 692-4175
laurieraphael@videotron.ca
Fresh market cuisine. Daniel Vézine, the chef and the owner, promotes innovative Québécois fare.

LE MARIE-CLARISSE
12, rue du Petit-Champlain
Quebec, PQ
Canada G1K 4H4
Tel: (418) 692-0857
Fax: (418) 692-5085
marie.clarisse@mediom.qc.ca
This 340-year-old house, situated in the oldest business district of America, offers guests a warm and romantic setting by the fireplace as they enjoy the fish and seafood specialties. Marie-Clarisse is the name of a boat constructed in 1922 that still sails the St. Lawrence River.

PINSONNIÈRE
124, rue Saint-Raphaël
Cap-à-l'Aigle
La Malbaie, PQ
Canada G5A 1X9
Tel: (418) 665-4431
pinsonniere@relaischateaux.com
This establishment on a lovely property overlooking the St. Lawrence River has a number of top-notch rooms, some with a rural décor, others more contemporary. The restaurant serves up innovative fare, created from fresh local and regional products: lamb and Muscovy duck from Charlevoix and Abitibi caviar. The dessert menu has some unusual offerings, such as bergamot-flavored crème brûlée or frozen zabaglione with ice cider.

SAINT-AMOUR
48, rue Sainte-Ursule
Quebec, PQ
Canada G1R 4E2
Tel: (418) 694-0667
Fax: (418) 694-0967
delice@saint-amour.com
Chef Jean-Luc Boulay travels around the world seeking flavors and scents to blend into the refined and subtle cuisine served at the restaurant, one of Quebec's best. The menu features a number of specialties, including foie gras from Quebec and an ice cream made from the La Marquise wine produced by the Orpailleur vineyards.

SAVEURS OUBLIÉES
350, rang Saint-Godefroy (route 352)
Les Éboulements, PQ
Canada G0A 2M0
Tel: (418) 635-9888
Fax: (418) 439-0616
This rural restaurant is also a farm; it serves its own organic vegetables and lamb. The farm sells a number of products, including jellies made from cedar, fir, St. John's Wort oil, and a pâté of lamb liver.

NATURAL SITES

APPALACHIANS
(Eastern Townships-Gaspé Peninsula)

JARDINS DE MÉTIS
200, route 132
Grand-Métis, PQ
Canada G0J 1Z0
Tel: (418) 775-2221
Fax: (418) 775-6201
jarmetis@jardinsmetis.com
The goal of the Jardins de Métis is to preserve the authenticity of the site. Certain plants and flowers that once flourished here have been reintroduced. These include the *gentiana ferreri*, which grew in the gentian avenue when the owner and gardener Elsie Reford lived here. Since 2000, the site has hosted the International Garden Festival. Every year, from late June to mid-September, the fertile garden is the venue for new ideas by famous landscape designers from Quebec and elsewhere.

PARC DE LA RIVIÈRE MITIS
900, route de la Mer
Sainte-Flavie, PQ
Canada G0J 2L0
Tel: (418) 775-2969/2221
Fax: (418) 775-9466
info@parcmitis.com
Visitors discover the magnificent landscape along the Mitis River, once one of the favorite spots of Elsie Reford (who designed the Jardins de Métis) for salmon fishing. The park was designed by

the well-known architect Pierre Thibault.

PARC NATIONAL DU MONT-MÉGANTIC
189, route du Parc
Notre-Dame-des-Bois, PQ
Canada J0B 2E0
Tel: (819) 888-2941
Fax: (819) 888-2943
parc.mont-megantic@sepaq.com
The Mont Mégantic observatory has the largest telescope in the eastern region of North America.

PARC NATIONAL DU MONT-ORFORD
3321, chemin du Parc
Canton
Orford, PQ
Canada J1X 7A2
Tel: (819) 843-9855
Fax: (819) 868-2107
parc.montorford@sepaq.com
With a surface area of nearly twenty-three square miles (sixty square kilometers), this park features a diverse landscape of mountains and hills covered with a mature maple forest. Visitors can hike and camp, while the more energetic can climb the mountain peaks.

PARC NATIONAL DE L'ÎLE-BONAVENTURE-ET-DU-ROCHER-PERCÉ
4, rue du Quai
C.P. 310
Percé, PQ
Canada G0C 2L0
Tel: (418) 782-2240

Fax: (418) 782-2241
parc.ibrperce@sepaq.com
The Rocher Percé and the Île-Bonaventure are the tail-end of the Appalachians as they drop into the icy waters of the St. Lawrence Gulf. The island is covered with wildflowers and dotted with a few signs of earlier habitation. It is now home to 223 different species of birds, including the sharp-shinned hawk and the second largest colony of gannets in the world.

PARC NATIONAL DE LA GASPÉSIE
900, route du Parc
Sainte-Anne-des-Monts, PQ
Canada G4V 2E3
Tel: (418) 763-3181
Fax: (418) 763-5435
parc.gaspesie@sepaq.com
This immense park stretches over three hundred square miles (eight hundred square kilometers) and has a large network of trails. It is also a great place to see some thirty species of mammals, including moose and caribou (in a rare occurrence, a herd of caribou has taken up residence in the park).

PARC NATIONAL FORILLON
122, bd Gaspé
Gaspé, PQ
Canada G9N 6T9
Tel: (418) 368-5505
Fax: (418) 368-6837
parcscanada-que@pc.gc.ca
This beautiful national park is located on the ocean. It's a

popular place among campers, who come for the lovely scenery and to observe black bears, seals, and whales.

LOWER ST. LAWRENCE

PARC DU BIC
Tel: (418) 736-5035
Seals are frequently spotted at this park, lounging on the many islands and reefs.

CÔTE NORD

PARC MARIN DU SAGUENAY-SAINT-LAURENT
From Saint-Fidèle to Tadoussac
(via the estuary road, route 138 from the west).
Tel: (418) 235-4703/ 4383
Unbelievable scenery and an equally impressive marine park, covering more than 380 square miles (1,000 square kilometers). Visitors may see a beluga in the Saguenay Fjord or a fin whale in the estuary of the St. Lawrence River. The region is a haven for 161 species of birds, including the common eider and the golden eagle.

ÎLES DE LA MADELEINE
No one can remain blasé about this archipelago. The best way to discover the islands is by bike or on foot, as most of the islands are linked by sandbars and

dunes. You can continue a tour aboard a small boat. The ecological reserve in Île Brion offers the most diverse flora. The Pointe-de-l'Est wildlife reserve on Grande Entrée is a protected territory and refuge for endangered migratory birds. For an overview of the archipelago, head to the top of Big Hill, the highest point on Île d'Entrée, a small island with a hundred or so English speakers of Scottish origin.

LAURENTIANS

PARC NATIONAL DU MONT-TREMBLANT
Chemin du Lac Supérieur
Lac Supérieur, PQ
Canada J0T 1P0
Tel: (819) 688-2281
Fax: (819) 688-6369
parc.monttremblant@sepaq.com
There are several places to enter this park (La Diable, Pimbina, L'Assomption, La Cachée, and Station Tremblant sectors). The park also has many observation points with overviews of the magnificent Laurentian forest, including the Lac Monroe belvedere.

MONTREAL

JARDIN BOTANIQUE DE MONTRÉAL
4101, rue Sherbrooke Est
Montreal, PQ
Canada H1X 2B2
Tel: (514) 872-1400
Fax: (514) 872-3765
jardin_botanique@ville.montreal.qc.ca

Montreal's botanical garden has been described, aptly, as one of the most beautiful in the world and one of the largest. It has 22,000 species of plants and flowers in all. The Chinese Garden has a number of pavilions, the Dream Lake and paths that are lined with lanterns during *The Magic of Lanterns*, a highly popular event held every autumn.

PARC DU MONT-ROYAL
Voie Camilien-Houde et Remembrance
Tel: (514) 843-8240
This natural park overlooks Montreal's downtown. It was laid out in the late nineteenth century by the landscape architect Frederic Law Olmsted, who also designed Central Park in New York. The "mountain" offers a wide range of activities, from strolls along paved paths to trails and cross-country skiing in the winter. The Chalet du Mont Royal at the top was constructed in a French Beaux-Arts style; it is the venue for many official events. The view from the belvedere in front of the chalet, overlooking the city and the St. Lawrence River, is spectacular.

ST. LAWRENCE PLAIN

DOMAINE JOLY-DE LOTBINIÈRE
Route de Pointe-Platon
C.P. 669

Sainte-Croix, PQ
Canada G0S 2H0
Tel: (418) 926-2462
domnjoly@globetrotter.net
The house, outbuildings, and gardens (with over two thousand species of plants) were designed in a romantic nineteenth-century style, making this property one of the most beautiful gardens and oldest forests in Quebec. The black walnut trees are magnificent. Owner Sir Henri-Gustave Joly de Lotbinière (who was Quebec's premier from 1878 to 1879) conducted a number of arboricultural experiments, planting two thousand black walnut trees, a species that usually grows in more southern climates. All that remain today are some one hundred trees, but they represent the oldest and most northern plantation of this type of deciduous tree in North America.

QUEBEC CITY AND REGION

CAP-À-L'AIGLE VILLAGE DES LILAS
762, rue Saint-Raphaël
La Malbaie, PQ
Canada G5A 2P2
Tel: (418) 665-2127
Fax: (418) 665-2679
villagedeslilas@qc.aira.com
A small village rated one of the most picturesque in Quebec.

PARC DE LA CHUTE-MONTMORENCY
2490, avenue Royale
Beauport, PQ

Canada G1C 1S1
Tel: (418) 663-3330
Fax: (418) 663-1706

montmorency@sepaq.com
This site opposite the St. Lawrence River and the Île

HOLIDAYS AND FESTIVALS

The dates of certain events may vary slightly from one year to the next.

January: Snow Festival (Montreal).
February: Winter Carnival (Quebec).
March: International Festival of Films on Art (Montreal).
April: Quebec International Book Fair,
May: International Interior Design Exhibition (Montreal).
June: Quebec Sea Festival (starts the weekend before Quebec's national holiday, June 24, and ends the weekend following the Canadian national holiday, July 1); Quebec National Holiday; Tadoussac Song Festival; Warwick Cheese Festival (Exhibition of Fine Cheese and the prestigious Sélection Caseus award); Mondial SAQ: fireworks in Montreal; Mosaicultures International (Montreal).
July: Canada Day, Quebec Summer Festival; Broad Bean Festival (Saguenay-Lac-Saint-Jean); Sand Castle Festival (Îles de la Madeleine); Petite-Vallée Song Festival (Gaspé Peninsula); International Arts Festival, Saint-

Sauveur (Laurentians); Montreal International Jazz Festival; Lanaudière International Festival (Plaine du Saint-Laurent); International Lac Saint-Jean Crossing (Saguenay-Lac-Saint-Jean); Fireworks Competition, (Quebec); International Symposium of Contemporary Art, Baie-Saint-Paul (Charlevoix); Tour des Arts-Studio Tour (Eastern Townships).
August: Nouvelle France Festival (Quebec); Blueberry Festival (Saguenay-Lac-Saint-Jean); World Film Festival (Montreal).
October: International Story-Telling Festival (Îles de la Madeleine); Snow Goose Festival (St. Lawrence Plain); International Festival of Traditional Arts (Quebec); International Festival of New Cinema and New Media (Montreal); Les Journées nationales du goût et des saveurs.
November: Salon cidres et saveurs du terroir (St. Lawrence Plain); International Book Fair, (Montreal).
December: Salon des métiers d'art du Québec (Montreal).

d'Orléans is exceptional. Visitors can approach on foot or take the cable car to the top of the falls to the Manoir Montmorency restaurant.

PARC DES CHAMPS-DE-BATAILLE
835, avenue Wilfrid Laurier
Quebec, PQ
Canada G1R 1L3
Tel: (418) 649-6157
Created in 1908, the Parc des Champs-de-Bataille is where visitors can discover the world of natural sciences and history, at the Maison de la découverte des plaines d'Abraham. It's hard to imagine that French and English soldiers fought in 1759 and in 1760 among these valleys and trees

overlooking the St. Lawrence River. The Plains of Abraham has become one of the city's favorite meeting places and a venue for cultural events and outdoor activities.

PARC NATIONAL DES HAUTES-GORGES-DE-LA-RIVIÈRE-MALBAIE
4, rue Maisonneuve
Clermont, PQ
Canada G4A 1L1
Fax: (418) 439-1228
parc.hautes-gorges@sepaq.com
This park is part of UNESCO's world network of biosphere reserves. The only way to reach this remote backcountry is from the

small town of Saint-Aimé-des Lacs.

RÉSERVE FAUNIQUE DE PORTNEUF
229, rue du Lac Vert
C.P. 10
Rivière-à-Pierre, PQ
Canada G0A 3A0
Tel: (418) 323-2021
Fax: (418) 323-2159
portneuf@sepaq.com
This wildlife reserve is filled with lakes and rivers, making this a fishing paradise for the speckled trout, brook trout, and muskie.

SAGUENAY-LAC-SAINT-JEAN

LES GRANDS JARDINS DE NORMANDIN
1515, avenue du Rocher

C.P. 567
Normandin, PQ
Canada G8M 4S6
Tel: (418) 274-1993
Fax: (418) 274-4994
grjard@qc.aira.com
The Grands Jardins de Normandin, situated north of Lac Saint-Jean, has much to offer visitors. These ornamental gardens, designed in keeping with the tenets of classical French gardens, feature parterres and a superb decorative vegetable garden inspired by the gardens of the Château de Villandry in France.

PARC NATIONAL DES MONTS-VALIN
360, rang Saint-Louis
Saint-Fulgence, PQ

Canada G0V 1S0
Tel: (418) 674-1200
Fax: (418) 674-1246
parc.monts-valin@sepaq.com
This park is situated in the heart of the Saguenay region. It is ideal for canoe trips and hiking. In the winter, a magical spot known as the Valley of Ghosts can get up to 16 feet (5 meters) of snow. The ghosts? These are the conifers, completely covered in snow. The only way to reach it on skis, snowshoes, or a tracked vehicle. There is also a trapper's cabin where you can warm up and get some food.

GETTING TO AND AROUND QUEBEC

AIR CANADA

When you want to travel to Quebec, the extensive Air Canada network will transport you there.
Air Canada offers:
- Two levels of service: Coach class, Business First class
- A VIP service at New York, Chicago, Denver, Los Angeles, and London Heathrow airports.
Thanks to these daily flights to Toronto and Montreal from the UK and the United States, Quebec and many other Canadian destinations can be at your fingertips.
UK—Tel: 0871 220 1111, Fax: 020 8750 8465
US—Tel: 1-888-247-2262
www.aircanada.com

To get to the Iles de la Madeleine during the summer months, you'll have to reserve your trip on the ferry (CTMA). You can take a boat from Montreal or drive to Souris. If you're in a hurry, you can also get to the islands by airplane. During the holiday season reserve your accommodation ahead of time.

GROUPE CTMA
The company offers cruises along the St. Lawrence from Montreal to the islands from early April to mid-October. In February and March, the boat leaves from Matane, on the Gaspé Peninsula.

CANADIAN EMBASSY—US
501 Pennsylvania Avenue, NW Washington, DC 20001
Tel: (202) 682-1740
Fax: (202) 682-7701
www.canadianembassy.org

CANADIAN HIGH COMMISSION—UK
Macdonald House
38 Grosvenor Street
London W1X 0AA
Fax: 020 7258 6506
ldn-cs@dfait-maeci.gc.ca

QUEBEC DELEGATION, BOSTON
31 Milk Street, 10th Floor
Boston, MA 02109

Tel: (617) 482-1193
Fax: (617) 482-1195
www.Quebec-Boston.org

QUEBEC DELEGATION, CHICAGO
444 N. Michigan Avenue
Suite 1900
Chicago, IL 60611
Tel: (312) 645-0392
Fax: (312) 645-0542

QUEBEC DELEGATION, LONDON
59 Pall Mall
London SW1Y 5JH
Tel: 020 7766 5900
Fax: 020 77930 7938
qc.londres@mri.gouv.qc.ca

BIBLIOGRAPHY

GUIDE BOOKS

Barlow, Julie and Austin Macdonald. *Montréal and Québec City for Dummies.* New York: Wiley, 2004.

Blore, Shawn and Herbert Bailey Livesey. *Frommer's Canada.* New York: Wiley, 2004.

Fletcher, Eric and Katharine Fletcher. *Quebec Off the Beaten Path: A Guide to Unique Places.* Guilford: Globe Pequot Press, 2002.

Gravenor, John David and Kristian Gravenor. *Montreal: The Unknown City.* Vancouver: Arsenal Pulp Press, 2003.

Gray, Jeremy. *Lonely Planet Montreal.* London: Lonely Planet, 2001.

Hustak, Alan. *Exploring Old Montreal: An Opinionated Guide to the Streets, Churches, and Historic Landmarks of the Old City.* Montreal: Véhicule Press, 2003.

Kay, Linda. *Romantic Days and Nights in Montreal.* Guilford: Globe Pequot Press, 2000.

Kokker, Steve. *Lonely Planet Quebec.* London: Lonely Planet, 2002.

Livesay, Herbert Bailey. *Frommer's Montreal and Quebec City 2004.* New York: Wiley, 2004.
Fodor's Montreal and Quebec City 2004. New York: Fodor's, 2004.
Michelin Green Guide: Quebec. 5th ed. Clermont-Ferrand: Michelin, 2003.
Michelin Must See Montreal. Clermont-Ferrand: Michelin, 2004.
Top 10 Montreal and Quebec City: Your Guide to the 10 Best of Everything. New York: Dorling Kindersley, 2004.

ILLUSTRATED BOOKS

Choko, Marc H. *Canadian Pacific Posters, 1883–1963.* Montreal: SIAP, 1999.

Dorion, Henri and Pierre Lahoud. *Quebec from the Air: From Season to Season.* Montreal: Éditions de l'Homme, 2004.

Huot, Claudel and Michel Lessard. *Québec: City of Light.* Montreal: Éditions de l'Homme, 2001.

Lacroix, Laurier. *Suzor-Coté: Light and Matter.* Ottawa: National Gallery of Canada, 2002.

Lessard, Michel. *Antique Furniture of Québec: Four Centuries of Furniture Making.* Toronto: McClelland & Stewart, 2002.

Marcoux, Yves. *Montréal: The Lights of My City.* Montreal: Éditions de l'Homme, 2000.

GASTRONOMY

Armstrong, Julian. *A Taste of Quebec.* New York: Hippocrene Books, 2001.

Ayanoglu, Byron. *Montreal's Best Restaurants.* Montreal: Véhicule Press, 2000.

Claman, Marcy. *Rise and Dine Canada.* Kirkland, Quebec: Callawind Publications, 1996.

Desjardins, Anne. *Anne Desjardins Cooks at L'Eau à la Bouche: the Seasonal Cuisine of Quebec.* Vancouver: Douglas & McIntyre, 2003.

USEFUL WEBSITES

www.bonjourquebec.com
www.sepaq.com

APPALACHIANS

www.bas-saint-laurent.org
www.destinationbeauce.com
www.saveursetcouleurs.com
www.tourisme-cantons.qc.ca
www.tourisme-gaspesie.com
www.saveursetcouleurs.com
www.tourisme-cantons.qc.ca
www.tourisme-gaspesie.com

LOWER ST. LAWRENCE

www.bas-saint-laurent.org

ÎLES DE LA MADELEINE

www.tourismeilesdelamadeleine.com

LAURENTIANS

www.icimauricie.com
www.laurentides.com
www.tourismepdh.org
www.tourisme-monteregie.qc.ca

MONTREAL

www.tourisme-montreal.org

ST. LAWRENCE PLAIN

www.destinationbeauce.com
www.tourisme-monteregie.qc.ca

QUEBEC

www.tourisme-charlevoix.com
www.tourismesaguenaylacsaintjean.qc.ca
www.veloroute-bleuets.qc.ca
www.ville.quebec.qc.ca

SAGUENAY-LAC-SAINT-JEAN

www.tourismesaguenaylacsaintjean.qc.ca
www.veloroute-bleuets.qc.ca

Duncan, Dorothy. *Nothing More Comforting: Canada's Heritage Food*. Toronto: Dundurn Press, 2003.

Secord, Laura. *The Laura Secord Canadian Cook Book*. Toronto: Whitecap Books, 2001.

Stewart, Anita and Robert Wigington. *The Flavours of Canada: a Celebration of the Finest Regional Foods*. Vancouver: Raincoast Books, 2000.
The All New Purity Cookbook: a Complete Book of Canadian Cooking. Toronto: Whitecap Books, 2001.

LITERATURE

Aquin, Hubert. *Blackout*. Toronto: House of Anansi Press, 1974.

Beaulieu, Victor-Lévy. *A Québécois Dream*. Toronto: Exile Editions, 1978.

Blais, Marie-Claire. *A Season in the Life of Emmanuel*. New York: Farrar, Straus, and Giroux, 1966.

Beauchemin, Yves. *Juliette*. Toronto: McClelland & Stewart, 1993.

Bourguignon, Stéphane. *Sandman Blues*. Toronto: Stoddart, 1996.

Cardinal, Marie. *In Other Words*. Bloomington: Indiana University Press, 1995.

Clavel, Bernard. *Castle of Books*. San Francisco: Chronicle Books, 2001.

Conan, Laure. *Angéline de Montbrun*. Toronto: University of Toronto Press, 1974.

Ducharme, Réjean. *The Daughter of Christopher Columbus*. Toronto: Guernica, 2000.

Ferron, Jacques. *The Cart*. Toronto: Exile Editions, 1980.

Godbout, Jacques. *The Golden Galarneaus*. Toronto: Coach House Press, 1995.

Hébert, Anne. *Children of the Black Sabbath*. Toronto: Musson Book Co., 1977.

Hébert, Anne. *Am I Disturbing You?* Toronto: House of Anansi Press, 1999.

Leclerc, Félix. *The Madman, the Kite, and the Island*. Ottawa: Oberon Press, 1976.

Lemelin, Roger. *In Quest of Splendor*. Toronto: McClelland & Stewart, 1955.

Lemelin, Roger. *The Plouffe Family*. Toronto: McClelland & Stewart, 1950.

Poulin, Jacques. *Autumn Rounds*. Toronto: Cormorant Books, 2002.

Proulx, Monique. *Aurora Montrealis*. Vancouver: Douglas & McIntyre, 1997.

Reyes, Alina. *When You Love You Must Depart*. London: Methuen, 1995.

Roy, Gabrielle. *Street of Riches*. Lincoln: University of Nebraska Press, 1993.

Savard, Félix-Antoine. *Master of the River*. Montreal: Harvest House, 1976.

Thériault, Yves. *Agoak: the Legacy of Agaguk*. Toronto: McGraw-Hill Ryerson, 1979.

Tremblay, Michel. *Birth of a Bookworm*. Vancouver: Talonbooks, 2003.

Vigneault, Guillaume. *Necessary Betrayals*. Vancouver: Douglas & McIntyre, 2003.

ESSAYS AND POETRY

Aquin, Hubert. *Writing Quebec: Selected Essays by Hubert Aquin*. Edmonton: University of Alberta Press, 1988.

Auf Der Mar, Nick. *Nick: A Montreal Life*. Montreal: Véhicule Press, 2003.

Borduas, Paul-Émile. *Writings: 1942–1958*. New York: New York University Press, 1978.
Grescoe, Taras. *Sacre Blues: An Unsentimental Journey Through Quebec*. Toronto: Macfarlane, Walter, and Ross, 2001.

Hémon, Louis. *Maria Chapdelaine: a Tale of the Lake St. John Country*. New York: Macmillan, 1924.

Hébert, Anne. *Day Has No Equal But Night: Poems*. Brockport: BOA Editions, 1994.

Hébert, Anne. *Selected Poems*. Toronto: Stoddart, 1988.

Miron, Gaston. *The Agonized Life: Poems and Prose*. Montreal: Torchy Wharf, 1980.

Nelligan, Émile. *The Complete Poems of Emile Nelligan*. Montreal: Harvest House, 1983.

Richler, Mordecai. *Home Sweet Home: My Canadian Album*. London: Hogarth Press, 1984.

Richler, Mordecai. *Oh Canada! Oh Quebec!: Requiem for a Divided Country*. New York: Knopf, 1992.

HISTORY

Brown, Craig. *The Illustrated History of Canada*. Toronto: Key Porter, 2003.

Dickinson, John A. and Brian J. Young. *A Short History of Quebec*. Montreal: McGill-Queens University Press, 2000.

Gillmor, Don and Pierre Turgeon. *Canada: A People's History*. Volume 1. Toronto: McClelland & Stewart, 2000.

Havard, Gilles. *The Great Peace of Montreal of 1701: French-Native Diplomacy in the Seventeenth Century*. Montreal: McGill-Queens University Press, 2001.

Mann, Susan. *The Dream of Nation: a Social and Intellectual History of Quebec*. Montreal: McGill-Queens University Press, 2003.

GLOSSARY

Middleton, William D. *The Bridge at Quebec*. Bloomington: Indiana University Press, 2001.

Stacey, C.P. *Quebec, 1759: the Siege and the Battle*. Toronto: Robin Brass Studio, 2002.

Trehearne, Brian. *The Montreal Forties: Modernist Poetry in Transition*. Toronto: University of Toronto Press, 1999.

Arrowhead sash: A hand-woven decorative accessory worn like a belt. The traditional arrowhead sash is the most beautiful example of the finger-weaving technique. They are still worn today during festivals and historical events.

Bélanger stove: Cast-iron wood-burning stove used for heating and cooking. Some had tanks for heating water.

Bleuet: Blueberry; also the nickname for people who live in the Lac-Saint-Jean region.

Cabouron: Small isolated hill in a plain. This term is used mostly in the Kamouraska region, where this geological feature is common.

Catalogne: A traditional bed-cover woven on a loom and consisting of thin strips of recycled fabric.

Cloudberry also salmou-berry: This fruit grows in the peat bogs of the subarctic region. The small orange berry looks like a raspberry.

Cookerie: The term used for a lumber camp kitchen.

Corten: High-density steel that only rusts on the surface.

Dépanneur: A small neighborhood store where you can buy cigarettes, newspapers, wine, beer, and basic foodstuffs. You can usually order by telephone and have your items delivered.

Dream-catcher: A circular-shaped talisman that First Nations peoples hang over their sleeping areas to ward off evil spirits.

Économuseum: The trademark name for a company that is a member of the Société internationale des entreprises Économusée®.

Grand Dérangement (Great Disturbance): This refers to the deportation of the Acadians from the St. Lawrence islands by the British authorities in 1755.

Goélette: Schooner, or sailing ship rigged with fore and aft sails on its two or more masts. The construction of these vessels was, up until recently, one of the traditional activities of the Île aux Coudres.

Ice wine: Wine made from grapes that have frozen on the vine, and are then picked and processed.

Innu: With the Cree, the Innu form the largest of Quebec's First Nations people (approximately 14,000). Until recently, they were called the Montagnais.

Inukshuk: A stone monument representing a human form and used as landmarks in the far north of Quebec.

Jeannois: Residents of the Lac Saint-Jean region.

Madelinot: Resident of the Îles de la Madeleine.

Maple taffy: Obtained by cooking then cooling maple syrup.

Messieurs du Séminaire: In Quebec, secular clergy belonging to an institution founded in the seventeenth century that included the Grand Séminaire (theology school) and the Petit Séminaire (secondary studies).

Musher: Dog-sled driver.

Muskellungeor Muskie: A large freshwater fish, similar to a pike.

Nordet: Northeast wind.

Ouananiche: Another name for the landlocked Atlantic salmon that live in Lac Saint-Jean.

Pourvoirie: An establishment that offers equipment for fishermen and hunters.

Queenzhy or nzhee: An igloo in the Malecite language.

Quiet Revolution: Starting in 1960, when an ambitious project of democratization, justice, and social equality was put in place, leading to profound changes in the Quebec society.

Rabaska: A large birch "bark" canoe, traditionally used on lakes and rivers by fur traders in the nineteenth century. *Rabaskas* are now usually made of fiberglass and are used for recreational purposes.

Sagamité: A traditional corn-flour soup.

Salange: Mist; a colloquial expression on the Îles de la Madeleine.

Sugarhouse: A small cabin in a maple forest in which the maple sap is transformed into maple sugar and syrup.

Tikinagan: A wood and fabric backpack, often decorated with beads and bright colors, used by First Nations peoples to carry their infants.

Tombolo: A strip of sand that links an island to the mainland or to another island, such as those formed by the *cabourons* in the Kamouraska region.

Tourtière: A pie made with ground pork and onions.

Voyageur: These people were explorers and merchants, working as guides on birch bark canoes plying the rivers of Canada during the conquest of the west.

PHOTOGRAPHIC CREDITS

All the photographs are by Philippe Saharoff, except: pages 10–11 © Daniel Faure/Agence Top; pages 14–15 © Hémisphères/Patrick Frilet; pages 32–33 © Daniel Faure/Agence Top; pages 44–45 © Hémisphères/Philippe Renault.

Translated from the French by Lisa Davidson

Copyediting: Chrisoula Petridis

Proofreading: Linda Gardiner

Color Separation: Quadrilaser

Distributed in North America by Rizzoli International Publications, Inc.

Previously published in French as *L'Art de Vivre au Québec*
© Éditions Flammarion, 2004
English-language edition
© Éditions Flammarion, 2004

26, rue Racine
75006 Paris

www.editions.flammarion.com

04 05 06 4 3 2 1

FC0457-04-IX
ISBN: 2-0803-0457-7
Dépôt légal: 09/2004

Printed in Italy by Canale

ACKNOWLEDGMENTS

Nathalie Roy and Philippe Saharoff would like to thank all those who contributed to this work, particularly Stéphane Allard, Mario Alarie, Léonard Aucoin and Cécile Théberge, Yves Bériault and Diane Decoste, Paulette Bilodeau and Paul-Eugène Roy, Linda and Gordon Black, Daniel Boucher, Colombe Bourque, Mark Brennan and Paule Vaillancourt, Louise Claude and Jean-Claude Lespérance, Isabel Crowell, Jacques Desbois, Hélène Desgagnés, David Dubreuil, and Serge Duval. Also Carole Faucher, Pierre Faucher, Dominique Gagnon and Édith Grégoire, Taras Iwanycki, Jacques Lachapelle (École d'architecture, Faculté de l'aménagement de l'Université de Montréal), Jean-Bernard Lambert (Institut de Tourisme et d'Hôtellerie du Québec); Martin Gagnon, Richard and Christiane Germain, Nathalie Grondin, Georges Mamelonnet, Arnaud Marande, Christine Marcoux, Gordon Moar, Marie-Andrée Mongeau and Jean Jasmin, and Daniel and Dominique Morin. Also Louise Nadeau, Diane Nadon (Ministère de l'Agriculture, des Pêcheries et de l'Alimentation du Québec), Lorraine Neault and Luce Savard (Parcs Canada, lieu historique national du Canada du Manoir Papineau). Christophe Nouaille, Mariette Parent, Louis Pauzé, Julie Payette, Nancy Picard and François Dubois, Benoît Pilon and Micheline Roy, as well as Christine Pryce, Alexander Reford, Marc Régnier, Claire Rémillard (Fondation des Seigneuries de l'Île-d'Orléans), Yves Savard, Stephen Stafford, André Tremblay, and, finally, Tina Tremblay.

They would also like to express their gratitude to architects Johanne Béland, Marie-Claude Hamelin and Loukas Yiacouvakis, Viateur Michaud, Stéphane Pratte, André Riopel, and Pierre Thibault; interior designers Madeleine Arbour, Jacques Bilodeau, Ana Borallo, Daniel Brisset, René Desjardins, Jean-Eudes Desmeules, Johanne Dunn, Michael Joannidis, and Serge Lafrance; and gifted craftsmen: Yvonne Bélanger, Mariouche Gagné, France Hervieux, and Alain Rhéaume.

They would also like to acknowledge the exceptionally helpful participation of interior designer Serge Lafrance and architect Jean Raymond throughout this entire project. And finally, Philippe Saharoff would like to extend special thanks to Henri Dorion, Dorothée Ghesquier, Nathalie Roy, and André Tremblay for the valuable research assistance that went into the creation of *Living in Quebec*.

The editors would like to thank Sylvie Ramaut, Juliette Hubert, and Célia Novak for their assistance with this book.

EDITOR'S NOTE

Within Quebec many places have both a French and an English name. The Natural Resources Canada database of Canadian geographical names served as our primary reference for place names throughout the text.

INDEX